Recipe for Success

Chef Tee's Journey from Prison to the Kitchen

Recipe for Success

Chef Tee's Journey from Prison to the Kitchen

Terrance "Chef Tee" Wallace

ISBN 979-8-9856725-0-3 (paperback)

ISBN 979-8-9856725-1-0 (ebook)

Visit the author's website at TurnAroundPlace.com

Published in the United States by Turn Around Place

Chesapeake, Virginia

Dedication

I want to give my friend and mentor, Chef Jimmy Hill, all my appreciation, because it was you who answered my jail house kite (internal message system) and gave me the opportunity to attend your classes, and it changed my life. I didn't understand at the time that you took on a life commitment with me, and you have been there with me from that day, helping me with character referencing, job referencing, organizations and partnerships that I would never have been able to be part of without your words. With a humble heart, I say thank you. I promise to carry on the fight for rehabilitation and second chances with the Turn Around Place.

Terry Wallace

Table of Contents

Childhood

1969-1979: ALABAMA

It was the early seventies, years before missing kids started appearing on milk cartons, back when doors were left unlocked and children minded themselves, roaming the streets in packs until dark. I was a baby, not even a year-and-a-half old, and my mother – now, I see she was barely more than a child herself – left me at home with an 'older' cousin who was not yet old enough to be left alone.

My cousin got hungry and maybe she thought that I wanted to eat too and she went into the kitchen and turned on the stove to fry some bologna for us as she had seen our moms do so often. Gurgling happily and teetering on my feet, barely able to talk or walk or even stand, I was next to her by the stove. Somehow, the sizzling grease splashed from the pan and onto my head.

I can't remember any of this because I was so young at the time but I imagine that the pain was excruciating, that I felt fear and felt unsafe because I didn't understand what happened or why. If I could remember exactly what I felt that day, maybe the kitchen wouldn't have become my sanctuary – or maybe, because my most formative moments occurred in kitchens, this path was always meant for me.

The top of my head would show the signs of neglect for the rest of my life and I have never been able to grow hair in those spots. In school when I was growing up, the other kids would pick on me and call me Patches because of the scars, so I would walk around with my hands covering the top of my head and later on hats to try to hide them.

It took a few days for the news of my head wrapped in bandages and ointment to make its way down the grapevine but my grandparents came to rescue me, driving up to my auntie's house in Birmingham where my mom and I were staying.

My Granddaddy was soft spoken for the most part, short with words but he was known to bust off a round and he came with his shotgun loaded. Simultaneously slamming the door and shooting into the air, Granddaddy exited his car with literal bangs. "Shug!" he barked, "Where's Terry at!"

His voice boomed loud and authoritative, ringing around the neighborhood, "All I want is Terry!"

I spent the rest of the early years of my childhood living with my grandparents and with them, life was grand. They lived deep in the country, about an hour away from Birmingham, Alabama and their home, perched on top of a hill in a wooded area overlooking the neighborhood, was the family hub.

The walls always hummed with life, with aunties and uncles and cousins and neighbors running and shouting and laughing and talking. The whole neighborhood felt like family, because even though we weren't related to each other, we came together and related *with* each other. They say it takes a village to raise a child and even though my mom was never around, there was never a shortage of laps to crawl into for a cuddle and I didn't know what I was missing out on.

Before he met Ma Dear, Granddaddy Neal had another family and had two kids with his first wife, Auntie Dean and my Uncle Neal, Junior. Ma Dear and Granddaddy Neal had four girls and a son: my mom, Shug; and my Aunties: Bird, Bobbie, and Deatrice; and my Uncle Bill. We had lived with Auntie Dean in the city but my aunts and uncles – and my mom – were barely more than kids themselves, with just 17 years between the oldest aunt and me, and I grew up with them like brothers and sisters.

My grandma, Ma Dear, was the sweetest woman I ever knew, with a soft round belly and dimples that filled her cheeks and eyes that crinkled at the corners when she smiled. Granddaddy Neal was half American Indian and half black, a little taller than Ma Dear but much skinnier, and he talked like a man born and raised in the south. I loved my grandfather. He was a locally well-known carpenter and he took me with him everywhere. When I was big enough, he even bought me a little tool belt and I would go to worksites with him and carry the nails and hammer. My Granddaddy was a hard worker and later someone would tell me a story about how he cut the tip off of his finger, wrapped it up, and kept right on working.

The two other people in the world who loved me just as much as Ma Dear and Granddaddy was my stepdad, Jimmy Lee Prince and his mother, Tha-Boo. I could count on one hand the number of times I saw them in the same room with my mother but they shared the responsibility of raising me along with my grandparents. On the weekends I would go to spend time with Jimmy and Tha-Boo and they lived in a whole other world in the inner city. Jimmy is the kindest soul I have ever known and to this day, I worked hard to reflect the lessons I learned from him in how I approach other people. He was dark skinned and muscular, a classy man who always dressed nice, all the way down to his shoes, even when he was just coming out to the country to pick me up. Compared to the pickup trucks that my neighbors all drove, the cars that he pulled up in seemed so fancy.

Ma Dear and Tha-Boo both worked for their entire lives in white people's homes as maids – back then, that was the way. I didn't learn about these things until much later but just a couple years before I was born, in 1960, Ruby Bridges was the first little black girl to go to school with white kids; in 1967, the landmark civil rights case of Loving v. Virginia ruled laws banning interracial marriages as unconstitutional; in 1968, Martin Luther King Jr. was assassinated.

When I was too small to be on my own, I remember riding the buses to run errands and go to work with whoever was keeping an eye on me. Their employers cooed over me and treated me good, often sending gifts home with my grandmothers for holidays and just because – sweaters and sweets and small toys. But I loved going with them to see the busyness of the inner city, all the cars and buses and people. We would get on the bus and through the window, I would watch our neighborhood and the countryside whizz past, and we would get off in a whole new world that hustled and bustled around me in ways it never could in the country. Much later I would master taking the bus by myself, opening up the world to anywhere I wanted to go.

Granddaddy Neal's house was on a hill at the top of East Scooter Road. When I was old enough, I would go exploring with my cousins and the other kids from around the block, running wild up and down the streets of the neighborhood until I knew each home and its inhabitants almost as well as my own. It was the type of place where you left the front door unlocked and neighbors who barely remembered to knock would invite themselves in for a chat and a bite of the fresh baked goods still cooling in the window.

Almost everyone had a garden in the backyard that supplied fresh fruits and vegetables in the spring and summer for us to can and preserve to save for fall and winter. We had every kind of tree you could possibly name: apples, figs, pears, plums, and pecans. There were watermelons growing on the vine, bushes bursting at the seams with strawberries, raspberries, blueberries. We had to throw rocks in the grass to make sure there were no snakes, pick carefully to avoid thorns and then eat *just* enough so that our bellies were filled with berries and faces stained in sweet juices. So many hours of my childhood were spent gardening with Ma Dear, learning how to take care of the plants so they grew strong and tall, when the best time to harvest them was, and what the techniques were to do it.

My cousin Deadman and I would keep an eye on what all our neighbors had growing in their gardens. All summer long we'd patrol the neighborhood for our prizes, whispering to each other, "When that watermelon get big enough, we gonna taste it!" A few times we were successful and we'd go somewhere in the woods to bust it open and eat till our stomachs were full to the top from eating watermelon. One of the times we got caught – and what a comedic sight it must have been, two kids just five and seven years old hauling a watermelon so big both of them had to carry it together – on our way out of Miss Palm's gardens. We both got whooped so hard we didn't forget about it until the following summer when the fruits were ripe for the taking again.

My mother would show up here and there to get me, maybe once a week, maybe every two weeks. Even as a child, I called my mother by her first name - not out of disrespect, but from a lack of affection. To me, she was just Shug. Calling her Mom didn't sound right, didn't feel right, it just didn't fit. When I was young, it enraged her that I called *her* mother Ma, instead of my own mother. I was in my thirties before I was able to call her *Mom*.

Whenever she popped up to take me to stay with her in the city, I would raise hell, kicking and screaming, "I don't wanna go with you! I don't want Shug!" over and over until Granddaddy Neal and Ma Dear would make her leave without me.

"When he's ready to go with you, we'll let him go," I overheard Granddaddy Neal saying to my mother once in his quiet angry voice that was somehow worse than when he was shouting, "As long as he's not wanting to go with you, we're not gonna force him to leave."

Even back then, I knew they were mad at her just like I was but I was too young to know or understand why. Shug was only 16 when she had me, literally still a child herself. It wasn't until much later that I found out that the deal was while her parents took care of me, she was going to Miles college to finish her teaching degree, and then she was supposed to come get me when she finished.

At the time, all I knew was that she was supposed to be around more than she was.

She ended up getting married after college and started building her life in the city and when I was around five, my sister Red, was born. My grandfather was firm in giving me a choice of where and who I spent my time with, and until then, I didn't want to be around Shug and her new family. But I began to grow curious of my new sister and so when she was around one years old, I started going to spend weekends with my mother.

I rarely saw her first husband while I was there. Even though Red was just a baby, she was the main reason I wanted to be around Shug or him. There were good moments too, because I remember lying on the floor with my sister in my mom's apartment, the sleepy afternoon sun filtering in through the windows and her tiny fat arms waving in the air as she gurgled happily. Ma Dear had taught Shug well and she could throw down in the kitchen. At her place for lunch, she'd make me grilled cheese sandwiches and for dinner, she'd fry up chicken with all the fixings

But Red was just a baby, and as babies do, she spent so much of her time crying, louder and louder, filling the room until there wasn't any space left for even your thoughts. And one time she cried so loud for so long that we were right there on the verge of tears with her, and finally Shug snapped and she slapped my sister so hard she knocked her out of the highchair she had been perched in. A cut appeared where she hit her head and she cried even harder, straining with the effort of wailing as much as her little lungs could handle.

The thing about head wounds is that they bleed really bad, even if it's not that serious. When Shug grabbed my sister, who was crying even louder now than before, she cradled her close to her chest and her shirt and hands were quickly stained red.

"Terry," she said, her voice high pitched and panicked. "You can't –" she grabbed my wrist, gripping me tight, "You can't tell anyone what I did." She made me pinky promise and my sister's blood smeared on my hand in the process. We took a cab to the hospital and Shug told the doctors that she rolled off the bed. All I could do was nod, wide eyed and terrified as they fixed her up.

I dreamed in shades of red for weeks afterwards and whenever Shug came for me, I would hide for as long as I could to delay the inevitable. Eventually, I managed to memorize the bus routes we took whenever she would succeed in taking me with her for the weekend. Filled with guilt and fear for leaving my sister with her, I would sneak away and escape, navigating the city busses that would drop me off at the gas station near my grandparent's house.

Growing up in Alabama, it was a rare moment – even as a growing boy – that I truly felt hunger. There was always hot food on the table, snacks in the pantry, a bowl of fruits from the garden in a bowl, or fresh baked goods cooling on the counter and a jug of ice-cold milk to wash it down with afterwards. Mostly we ate barbeque: ribs, ham, and pork chops, fried chicken, or fish, with sides like mac and cheese, mashed potatoes, and collard greens. Corn bread and dinner rolls and biscuits were always steaming from the oven, slathered in a thick layer of butter or honey that came from a local farm a few miles away. Almost the entire family came together around the table to share every meal, and they were noisy affairs, with loud discussions and everyone trying to talk and shout and laugh over each other.

Like clockwork at every meal, Granddaddy would scowl and shake his finger at his son, my Uncle Billy, and he'd shout, "It seems that Billy is the captain of this ship – Captain Billy! He gets the first piece of cornbread; he gets first choice of the chicken wings!" his voice rising above the rest of ours accusingly. Billy was Ma Dear's pride and joy, her only son, but Granddaddy Neal didn't see him as that. Billy didn't like to feed the hogs, pick vegetables, or cut the wood. He wouldn't do his chores and they would fall on anyone else who had the misfortune to be in the vicinity. Granddaddy Neal thought that Ma Dear was spoiling him into a lazy man who lacked a work ethic, because she let him get away with anything and would defend him under any circumstances. He couldn't stand it, and he was vocal about it. "He's a growing boy, Neal," Ma Dear would shush him with a smile from her spot at the table as she piled another fixing onto Billy's plate.

I was never a picky eater but I remember being five years old at Jimmy's place – he could throw down in the kitchen just as hard as anyone else in my family, but it was the first time I'd ever seen fish cooked in a way that wasn't deep fried. I watched him make a red snapper Papillote, where you wrap the whole fish, head and all, with spices and onions, and garlic and lemons, together in tin foil and bake it slowly. Even after it was finished cooking and he had removed the fish head and even though it smelled good and my stomach was rumbling, I remember hollering, "I don't want none of that!" Jimmy only had to patiently threaten me once with eating this cold for breakfast if I didn't eat it now for dinner, before I doubtfully took a small bite in my mouth. I never second guessed anything he made for me again after that.

Once in a while when I was in the city, I'd get to eat McDonalds or Burger King, which seemed like a treat at the time. But at home, our food was always fresh, farm to table long before it became a trend, with vegetables we'd grown and meat we'd raised ourselves and cooked with so much love by my grandmothers. Ma Dear's country kitchen was spacious, with miles of counter space and cupboards and a pantry hiding all sorts of goodies; Tha-Boo's apartment kitchen was smaller but just as cozy, every nook and cranny in her fewer cupboards crammed to make up for the lack of space. When I was little, I'd crowd around them in their kitchens, clinging to their legs and begging, "Please, I wanna help stir the pots!" and "Just a little taste, please!" Later on, they would carefully teach me how to chop vegetables, season the meat, and build a sauce, fearless in the kitchen despite the scars on the top of my head.

The Shot House was the local bar – somebody's house where they converted most of the living spaces into a bar. It was definitely illegal but everybody who lived in the country gathered there to drink and blow off steam, including all the local firefighters, nurses, cops, judges, and attorneys. It was normal for parents to take their kids with them to the Shot House where they could buy beers and shots of whiskey for themselves, and candy, potato chips, and soda for the kids. You could get a line of credit so that you could drink until pay day and every Friday without fail, people would show up to pay their bill and start the week afresh.

While the adults would drink, smoke, and play dominos and cards, the woods in the back were our playground. At some point, somebody had hung swings from some large branches for us. We'd play hide and seek and tag between the trees, and in the dirt, we drew boxes and rings for hopscotch and shooting marbles. We would jump rope and wrestle, and throw baseballs and footballs until the stars came out to twinkle and the voices of our parents started calling for us to get a move on towards home.

Granddaddy Neal was a regular at the Shot House and more often than not, he'd bring me along with him. One time when I was around six, he bought two candy bars for me and fire water for himself. The candy bars were much bigger back in the day, hanging out of my pockets like two pistols. While I minded myself and played with the other kids, Granddaddy Neal sat at a table with his friends laughing and drinking. The candy bars disappeared into my belly almost as fast as he bought them for me and by the time we had to leave, he was staggering around, barely able to stay on his feet.

The lady who ran the place wouldn't let him drive home. She remembered that Granddaddy used to bring my aunties to the Shot House when they were little. "Does your babe still want that pony out back?" she asked with a kind laugh in her voice and Granddaddy Neal narrowed his drunken bloodshot eyes at her and grinned widely, always ready to do anything to please us. She struck a deal to exchange the car for the pony so Granddaddy could walk off his buzz and get us home safe.

Granddaddy Neal put me on the back of the pony, patting its neck absently. All the way home I bounced along and laughed as he puffed his chest out and said with drunken boom, "This here pony is for your Auntie Bird!"

We walked up the hill together and how the neighbors must have laughed at my grandfather staggering drunk with me perched on the back of the pony. We got to the house and Granddaddy started to call for my Auntie Bird to come outside so he could show her something. "Birdy!" he shouted from the lawn, "Where's my baby Bird?"

Ma Dear yelled from inside, "Neal, you been drinking!" and Granddaddy Neal replied while gesturing to me with his finger over his lips and a wink, "Why would you say such a thing? I swear I haven't touched the stuff!"

Aunt Bird came outside with her robe wrapped around her and looked around, concerned. "Daddy, where's the car? You gonna make me late for work in the morning!"

"I got you a pony!" he exclaimed with glee, leaning side to side and arms outstretched like he was showing her what she had won in a gameshow.

My auntie just shook her head. "Daddy, I wanted a pony when I was 10! I can't ride that pony to work!" Ma Dear called the Shot House to see where the car was and the lady told her that they just wanted Granddaddy to get home safe with me. Our station wagon was parked right where he left it. Boy, them was the good old days in Alabama.

Since we lived so far into the country, we had a gas station where you could fill up your tank and buy single cigarettes, but there was really nothing around us and it was a trek to the nearest grocery store. People stocked their pantries well with staples like flour and grew and preserved their own fruits and veggies, buying meat from local farmers to avoid unnecessary trips to buy groceries. Once a week or so, a truck – kind of like a rolling Wal-Mart – would come with electronic items and anything else we might need to stock up on.

Other than that, some families would buy extras of certain supplies to sell on to the rest of the neighborhood, operating little stores out of their home. That was just how Southern black people did back then. My favorite store was at Miss Palm's house and the kids in the neighborhood affectionately nicknamed her 'The Candy Lady' because she sold candy, sodas, and single serving sized bags of potato chips. We all wanted to do her favors like cut her grass and take out her trash: that's how we learned that we had to work for what we wanted at a young age.

Miss Palm was friendly with Ma Dear, but her husband Mr. Palm was always mad at Granddaddy Neal because he would get drunk at the Shot House every weekend and more often than not, run down the mailboxes on his way home. Mr. Palm would cuss him out every time until Granddaddy took his toolbox to the top of the hill and rebuild all the mailboxes, grumbling under his breath. But Miss Palm always had Baby Ruth, Sugar Daddy, and Now & Later candies that she would give us with a wink in exchange for our pennies whenever we came knocking on her door.

Uncle Billy and our cousin Frank were around 13 years older than me, and they were always scheming and getting into trouble together. They knew that I wanted badly to be a part of their 'games'. One day, Billy had found me playing by myself and said temptingly, "Wrong Foot, you want some candy?" They called me Wrong Foot because I still had trouble telling the difference between right and left and was always putting my shoes on the wrong foot.

"Yes!" I exclaimed but I had overheard Miss Palm telling Ma Dear that she was going to visit her family in another city and I told him sadly, "But the Candy Lady ain't at home."

"Yeah, but she said that she left some candy on the table for you, we just have to go get it!" they reassured me with wide grins, knowing fully well that I was young and trusting. I was overjoyed they wanted to include me in something and convinced by the thought of sweet chocolate melting on my tongue.

At Miss Palm's house, they didn't go to the front door, leading me instead to the small side window that was cracked for ventilation. I said, "Y'all going the wrong way. The door's over here!"

"I lost the key she gave me, Wrong Foot," Captain Billy said, "You got to go through the window to open the back door so we can get you the candy."

The window was too narrow for them, but I was just the right size to fit in. While I stood there trying to figure out what to do, Billy pushed the window wider and Frank grabbed me by the waist. Together, they hoisted me up like a sack of apples and in I went through the window.

The house was still and quiet inside. For a moment I squinted into the dim light trying to sense where my prize would be. "Open the back door!" their voices urged through the window, but the lock on the door was still too high for me and I couldn't reach it. "Wrong Foot, go get a chair and get the door open or you ain't getting no candy." The idea of that sugary goodness was motivation enough. I wanted that candy.

I got the door open and Captain Billy and Frank came rushing in. The Palm's had a brand-new color TV, which was better than the candy in their eyes. They told me they couldn't find the candy and took the TV to the rear of the house, making sure the door was shut tight behind us on the way out.

I was mad for the rest of the day. Ma Dear seen me pouting and she always knew when something was wrong. In her sweet voice she asked me, "What's wrong, baby?"

"Billy didn't get me no candy," I pouted.

"Billy *can't* get you no candy," she corrected. "Miss Palm ain't at home."

"I told him that, mama, but they put me in the window to get the candy and the only thing they got was the TV." I didn't know what I was saying – I didn't necessarily mean to tell on them, but I was pissed I didn't have no candy.

"Boy, what'd you say?" Ma Dear demanded.

I said, "Billy and Frank got the TV from Miss Palm, mama." Her eyes were wider than I'd ever seen and she looked like she might spit. "They didn't get me no candy though."

When Billy came in later that evening Ma Dear didn't even wait until he had shut the door to start on him. "That TV is going back before your daddy finds out about this!" she yelled, just about as mad as she had ever been. Ma Dear managed to get the TV back to Miss Palm when she returned from Alabama and she begged her not to tell but the rumors started flying around and word of Captain Billy stealing the TV would hit the Shot House.

The truck-store rolled into the neighborhood and Ma Dear and I walked there one afternoon a few days after the TV was returned. We weren't even gone for an hour but when we returned, to our surprise, Granddaddy was home and he had Billy tied to a chair, hollering and cussing at him.

A few weeks before, Billy had fed the hogs glass to kill them so he could get out of his chores, robbing us of our main source of meat for the winter. Billy was already on thin ice, and if that wasn't bad enough, what really set Granddaddy Neal off was that he heard whispers at the Shot House that Billy had taken me on my first breaking and entering.

Granddaddy hated a liar and he hated a thief and somehow Captain Billy had turned out to be both. He was humiliated and enraged by the thoughtlessness of Billy's actions and he beat him almost the whole time we were gone before he tied him to the chair. Ma Dear was screaming, "Please Neal, don't kill him!" and Billy was crying and bucking, eyes as big as silver dollars.

I was just little and I thought they were playing a game. I started patting my hands to my mouth, making Indian war cries. "Kill him, Granddaddy, kill him!"

"Terry, be quiet!" Ma Dear snapped at me sharply for possibly the first time in my life, shutting me up instantly.

Granddaddy Neal's wrath was loud like thunder and he said to Ma Dear, "This the worst thing you ever did, bringing him into the world," gesturing at Billy in the chair. "God ain't pleased with you for bearing a sorry-son-of-a-bitch like Captain Bill."

His words shook the house as though they came from God himself. All of a sudden, the fight disappeared out of him and he looked defeated and sad. "I love you so much, woman," he said, much quieter now. "But this boy is the worst thing you ever done. I can't keep you warm at night, honey, because Captain Billy didn't chop the wood. I can't feed you because Captain Billy killed the hogs. And now, the SOB has turned my grandbaby into a thief."

Ma Dear had been screaming so loud that Granddaddy Neal was interrupted by the neighbors coming to see what all the noise was about. Billy was released from his chair and somehow – that was the end of that.

Usually, clothing and shoes were passed from cousin to cousin until it was too worn out to be fixed and you could practically see through the middle. But one afternoon, I was in the city running errands with Ma Dear and we walked past a shoe store. I saw a pair of purple high-top All Star sneakers in the window – my favorite color back then – and I was instantly smitten. I begged and begged her for them and before we got on the bus to go back home, she took me back and bought me my very own pair. I put them on my feet and tossed my old hand-me-downs into a bag, strutting proudly out of the shoe store like a peacock.

When we got home, my cousin Deadman was waiting for us on the porch. He jumped up and waved when he saw us coming up the hill. "Look what I got!" I shouted at him, letting go of Ma Dear's hand to run the rest of the way to the house. Deadman and I were just a few years apart and in our hearts, we were brothers. He was a few years older and he was slicker than me, but we spent almost all our time together, playing games and probably irritating the hell out of our older cousins.

"Those look fast, Tee!" he said, whistling admiringly as I kicked up one foot and then the other, showing off my brand-new shoes. "We gotta race and see how fast they make you!"

None of my other cousins brought out the competitive streak in me like Deadman. We were always finding new ways to compete and try to one up the other – Ma Dear liked to draw the line at eating competitions, swatting us over the head and reminding us to mind our manners.

We set up a race on the street, using chalk to draw starting and finishing lines. A group of our friends and other cousins had gathered to watch, and one would call out, "On your marks…get ready…get set…gooooo!" from the sideline.

Even though I always came last, I had really thought my new kicks would give me an edge. "It's 'cause I've got *fast* shoes," Deadman told me after he beat me, panting as we walked back to the finish line.

"What you mean?" I asked, eyes narrowed as I inspected his feet.

"My shoes help me run faster!" he said like it was obvious. "That's how I always beat your ass."

I sat down on the pavement in disbelief and started undoing the laces of my new shoes, pulling them off my feet. "Let me try your shoes," I demanded.

He toed off his old, beat-up sneakers and sat down on the ground next to me as we put on each other's shoes. "These don't feel fast at all."

"I got you this time!" I shot back confidently, bouncing up and down in place as we took our positions to start another race.

I took off with everything I had like a firecracker. His shoes were flapping and coming apart at the seams, but Deadman put on a convincing show and I crossed the finish line just before he did — usually, I lagged a few seconds behind, and beating him so narrowly felt glorious.

"Winner gets to keep the fast shoes," I declared afterwards. How had I never known that it was the shoes that made Deadman faster than me? I wanted to keep this advantage. He protested a little, but he had played his part well and I refused to take his old shoes off my feet. He went home wearing my *new* shoes and I went home with my chest poked out, victorious with Deadman's fast shoes.

I barely walked through the door when Ma Dear gave me a once over and saw the ratty sneakers on my feet. "Baby, what happened to your shoes?"

"I traded my new shoes for fast shoes!" I explained to her gleefully.

"Boy, what are you talking about," she moved towards me to take a closer look. "You haven't even had them for a whole day! Where are your new shoes?"

No matter how many different ways she asked me, I wouldn't give in to her interrogation tactics because I wanted to keep these fast shoes so I could keep beating

Deadman. No matter what way Ma Dear came at me, she could not get me to crack.

But Granddaddy knew what time it was and he knew exactly what to say. He heard me tell Ma Dear that I traded them for 'fast shoes' and he realized that I had been slicked out of my shoes and that he had to take a slick approach to get me to confess what happened. He came and sat close to me and asked, "Terry, who did you trade your slow shoes to?"

I still wouldn't give in, but Granddaddy never broke a sweat. He kept an even tone and gave me another game, another way of seeing the situation. He told me that my shoes were new and maybe they were slow now, but the more that I wore them, the faster they would get. Deadman hadn't told me that part. I realized that I had been tricked out of my new shoes. If I had known that they would get faster, I wouldn't have made the trade.

I was furious and I went marching down the street to get my new shoes. I went to Deadman's house and banged on the door until my auntie answered. When Deadman came to the door, I told him to give me my shoes.

"Nuh-uh," he said. "You traded me them, fair and square!" Then he looked past me and saw Granddaddy who had followed me, just standing on the driveway with his arms crossed over his chest. Deadman went inside for a moment and then came back and wordlessly handed me my shoes.

It's almost embarrassing how long it took me to realize that there was never anything fast about anyone's shoes

– Deadman just had longer legs than me and I needed a growth spurt to even us out. It took me longer to understand that Deadman and Granddaddy had both engaged in psychological warfare to get me to do what they wanted.

When I was 10 years old, my mom's second husband Willie Earl convinced her to move to Michigan. Shug had divorced her first husband and married Willie Earl the previous year after he got her pregnant with twins. Now she was pregnant again with her fifth child, and had decided that I was her responsibility and they came to take me away from my grandparents who had been raising me since I was a baby.

Willie Earl was tall and thin, brown skinned with dark eyes that seemed to shine too bright. I had only seen him a few times here and there when I was at visiting, but Granddaddy didn't like him, so I didn't go around him that much. That Christmas, Ma Dear and Granddaddy and Tha-Boo and Jimmy had given me twenty dollars, which was a lot of money back then. I went to see my mom, my sister, and the new twin babies, Biddy and Beakman, a few days later. Willie Earl was there and he overheard me telling them about my Christmas present and proceeded to slick talk me out of it. It caused a huge commotion when I got back home and Granddaddy heard that a grown man had slicked his grandson out of his money. He went down and raised hell but I never did get my twenty bucks back.

Willie Earl and my mom loaded my three siblings into the car and in the middle of the night, they showed up at my grandparent's home to get me. I was pulled out of bed, instantly alert at the way Ma Dear hugged me tight, then haphazardly shoved my shoes into my hands and some of my clothes into a backpack. "Don't trust this man with your babies!" I remember hearing Granddaddy Neal through the open door, begging Shug not to take his grandchildren. "He abandoned his family before Shug," he said, his voice laced with warning. "He'll do it again." She pushed past Granddaddy and with deceptive strength, picked me up and took me out of the house, packing me kicking and screaming into the car. The noise woke my sleeping siblings who cried with me.

The tires pulled out of the driveway with a screech and as I watched tearfully through the rearview window, my grandparents and their home got smaller and smaller. I could barely blink or even breathe as the neighborhood and all of its familiar houses and trees and streets disappeared from my sight.

I didn't know where we were going but I was already plotting my escape, filled with thoughts of finding the nearest bus station to make my way home. In my head, I was taking notes, sullen as I watched the signs flitting past on the highway, illuminated beacons sticking out in the darkness. But they drove for so long that I couldn't keep track and eventually, I fell asleep. When I woke up, I was still mad and still didn't know where we were, except that the world outside the car windows looked different and new and like we were very far away from home. When we stopped for bathroom breaks and to stretch our legs, we shivered, our breaths puffing out in clouds on the frigid air. Within a day, we had arrived.

1979-1982: MICHIGAN

It was deep winter when we got there and we were in Lansing, Michigan during the Blizzard of 1979. I had never been this far north before. We were staying with Willie Earl's brother, who had a wife and 2 kids of his own, so we were nine people crammed in a three-room apartment. My first responsibility in Michigan was to take care of the twins. They were just babies – I fed them bottles, changed their diapers, put them to nap, played with them, everything.

It had been a week since we had seen Willie Earl and I remember creeping between the rooms, trying to take up as little space as possible and feeling tense and out of place. He had taken us across the country and then abandoned us. At the time, my mom wouldn't tell us where Willie Earl was or what he was doing, but looking back, he was most likely cheating or getting high.

Whenever the state of Michigan is mentioned, Detroit is pretty much the only place people not from there know about. Detroit was known for being a major car manufacturer with Ford and General Motors. Detroit was also known as Motown: the heart of rhythm and blues.

But anybody from Michigan is very familiar with Lansing, the headquarters and capitol of Michigan. It was a small city eighty eight miles west of Detroit, with a lot of money back in the day. Detroit made parts for GM and Ford, but Lansing was where Cadillacs and Chevys were made.

If you were to ask anybody who lived there today, I guarantee most would say their grandmothers and grandfathers came from the south with roots from the Bible Belt. People from the South migrated up North to escape poverty, Jim Crow laws, and segregation, hoping for what Southerners considered 'living the dream of the white man's world' - a world where racism didn't exist and black men made the same wages as a white man working side-by-side every day.

Back in those days, most black men didn't know how to read or write. Knowing how to read or write wasn't a requirement to work on the assembly line. Willie Earl was one of those men, and on the word of his brother who was already living and working there, had gotten a job at the Oldsmobile factory producing parts for the booming car industry. He sold Shug his dream: hook, line, and sinker. She had a bachelor's degree and dreamed of being a teacher and she let a man who didn't even have a GED slick her out of her dream and move her to another state.

Shug carried a sense of shame and sadness with her like weights: she had left her home and her family – as rocky as their relationship could be - for *this?*

We had been away from Alabama for less than two weeks and did not have proper clothing for a Michigan winter. My feet were freezing in the purple Converse that I had shoved on when they took me in the middle of the night and our coats were thin and let the icy wind blow right through us. Despite all this, she made up her mind to take us and leave Willie Earl's brother's house. We walked through the snow, going towards the station with some half-baked plan in Shug's head of getting us on a bus back home to Alabama.

An older white lady pulled her car over to the side of the road and rolled her window down to check on us, concern creasing her kind features. We were a sad, shivering group of six: I was the oldest child, holding my Beakman and Biddy, the twins, in my arms. Shug was heavily pregnant, grasping the hand of her my sister Red.

When the lady asked us where we were going, I remember being shocked to see Shug's face crumbling, tears leaking down her face. We didn't have any family or friends there in Michigan, and as angry as I was to even be there in the first place, it wounded me to see her hurt like that.

The lady told Shug that we were walking in the wrong direction and she leaned over the seat to open the passenger door, inviting us into her warm car.

She let us stay in her home for two weeks where we felt safe, warm, and fed for the first time in weeks. Her house was bigger than anything I'd ever lived in, nestled away in a nice neighborhood and having lived my whole life in the south, I had never been this up close and personal with a white person for such extended periods of the time before. She was soft spoken and gentle, and she got us new boots and thick, warm clothes more suited to a Michigan winter. As an adult, I would later retrace the steps of my childhood and remember her kind heart.

As though by divine intervention, the lady just happened to be a member of the Board of Education. When she found out that Shug had a degree in Education and had been a substitute teacher in Alabama, she committed herself to helping my Mom get back on her feet. In the two weeks we stayed with her, she helped my Mom find housing and furniture and we all felt a sense of hope and ease.

This feeling was short-lived and didn't last long. Almost as soon as we were settled in our own new home, my baby brother, KJ, was born and Willie Earl weaseled his way back into our lives. For the next five years, Shug depended on welfare and Willie Earl's handouts. They manipulated the system, with him working at Oldsmobile full time while she was getting assistance. Even though the lady who helped us had found her a job, Willie Earl would not allow her to work as a way of controlling her. He started beating on her from time to time and that's when she really began to drink.

Moving to Michigan meant that Shug lost her family and support system. She could have owned up to her mistakes and returned to them in Alabama at any time, but Shug and her siblings had a mostly friendly rivalry; she was full of pride and didn't want to admit that she had been wrong and be seen as a failure in their eyes. At heart, she was a sweet country girl, who had been slick-talked out of her dreams by a city slicker. Whatever mixed feelings I'd had about her as a young child in Alabama were only intensified by how Michigan turned out to be. I understand now it's because she knew that she was living beneath her potential. Shug had lost sight of her old self and became overwhelmed by the anger and bitterness of her own choices.

It didn't take long for her to turn the energy into beating on my siblings and me. Sometimes she whooped us out of our sleep. We went from being terrified of him beating her and seeing him as a monster to being forced to see Willie Earl as our savior when he shielded us from our mother's vicious unprovoked beatings. I wasn't used to this — the angry shouting, the beatings, the violence. I had gone from arms outstretched in love, ready for a hug and cuddle, to arms ready for battle.

Sometimes Shug got creative with ways to punish us too. When my youngest siblings were fussing, she would invent new chores for us, like picking the lint off carpet with our fingers as though we were vacuum cleaners. My brothers and sisters would be crying, sniffling the whole time and I'd find ways to make games out of it, whispering, "Hey, bet you guys can't make a bigger pile than me!" until their tears dried up, distracted by the determination to win.

It was a blessing when we started school. I appreciated the chance to get away from Shug and surrounded by kids my age who eventually became my friends; I could almost forget that I had been dragged away from my home and dropped into a hostile environment. But more than that, I made sure to be at school every single day so I could be first in line because it gave me a chance to *eat*.

The food in Michigan was different. I was skinny for a long time after we moved because the food just didn't taste right to me – dinner was often soggy baloney sandwiches with welfare cheese, hotdogs, mushy vegetables, and canned chili. Gone were the days of the family caring for and growing the food we ate. My stomach knotting on itself, grumbling in incessant hunger was an uncomfortable new reality to face.

There was no space for a garden here and the weather only really allowed for it half the year anyway. Until food stamps, I hadn't even realized how many different foods were available that was processed – I thought that everybody grew and preserved their own veggies. Most of the time, the cupboards were empty and the hot meals we did eat at home had a distinct flavor of tin, leftover from the cans they came in, no matter how many seasonings got thrown on top.

Once or twice a week when Willie Earl was off work and at home, Shug would actually make a homemade meal for us, almost making me forget how much had changed. She could still throw down in the kitchen when she wanted to and I'd stand by her side at the counter, trying to help and learn what she was doing. But Shug started seeking happiness outside of our home, making friends with other bored housewives and suddenly we saw her less and less – somehow, that enraged her more. She would yell at us for an hour or two after we got home in the afternoon and then she would go out with them, drinking and cackling away in one of their kitchens or playing bingo, and then she wouldn't come home until almost midnight.

Those nights, my siblings and I learned to barricade the door to the room we shared, blocking the entrance with furniture so she wouldn't come beat us out of our sleep. At least then, we could hear her coming, because she'd pound on the door with her fists and body, seemingly unable to tire herself out as she'd shout, "Open this door – open this door – open this goddamn door *right now!*" until finally we'd move the things away and let her in, trying to shield ourselves and each other from her fists.

We had settled in the west side of Lansing in the Brickyard Projects. Everyone in the projects had something in common: we were all poor. We were all from different parts of the world: migrants from the south, and then there were Arabs, Mexicans, Africans, Vietnamese…I had never even heard of some of these places.

Most of the kids I knew had parents who had come to Lansing to work in the car factories. During the first couple of years, I used to run wild in the streets with a pack of boys. The Weginka brothers – Charles, a boy my age, great at both singing and also basketball and his younger twin brothers, Stacey and Tracey – had come straight out of Tennessee and were seen as PWT: Poor White Trash. Nigel was a lanky dark-skinned kid whose parents had recently moved across the ocean from Nigeria.

The Weginka brothers were raised in the South and used to being around black people, but being friends with white kids was new to me and definitely new to Nigel. His father had a superiority complex and used to preach in heavily accented English that Africans were better than black Americans because we didn't know where we came from. Charles got a kick out of winding him up and they were always arguing.

Every time we would get close to Nigel's house, his father would start shouting at us, *Akata! Akata! Akata!* Eventually we found out what *Akata* meant: it was a slur, describing us as black American cotton pickers and I realized that it was geared mostly towards me.

Charles would tease him and call Nigel a nigga, trying to defend me in a twisted way. Nigel would beat his chest and fire back full of pride, "I ain't no nigga, I am from *Africa.*"

Despite our differences we stuck together all throughout middle school since we shared a unifying bond: we all had similar situations going on at home and we were always left out by default because we never had money for field trips. Our teachers didn't even want to waste paper on us and wouldn't stop at our desks with permissions slips.

Sometimes Shug would kick me out for talking back and as much as it hurt my pride, I was always welcome to stay with either the Weginka brothers or Nigel. It didn't take us long to figure out that nobody cared if we skipped classes. Most days, we would go in just for the lunch period, but one afternoon we were all still hungry, with no money and no food at home in the fridge. Charles asked us in an offhanded drawl, "Do y'all know how to steal from the store?" He was the leader in this pack, with an easy-going smile and a sharp mind that was always quick to devise a plan.

Me and Nigel would go into the store first. The brothers followed us in shortly after to do the distracting: Charles would talk to the clerk, asking all sorts of questions, and Stacy and Tracy would walk around causing a ruckus. Since the three of them were white, the clerk wouldn't suspect a thing. Meanwhile, Nigel and I walked around quietly slipping snacks into our pockets and then out the front door. Afterwards, we met in the alley around the corner and divided our plunder amongst ourselves. Nigel didn't like the fact that we would handle the riskiest part and do all the stealing while Charles would get first pick of the goods, but wolfing down the stolen candy bars tasted so good, I couldn't quite bring myself to agree.

Stacy and Tracy were just a sharp as their brother and another time we skipped class, they hatched a plan. Instead of us all sitting around, hungry and poor, they put us in the direction of the local university campus. The twins had come prepared: when we got there, they handed me a big black trash bag and I watched them start collecting pop cans that were littered on the lawns, pulling them out of trash cans and shaking out the excess liquid. Between the five of us, in no time, we had these huge bags filled with cans and we dragged them to the recycling center.

Once they were weighed, I had earned my first dollar. I was instantly hooked: the idea of having control of my own money was sweeter than any stolen candy bar and to this day, I am grateful to those kids who taught me to hustle. As we got older, we each found our own crowds and branched off to do our own thing, but we had grown up together.

Seeing Shug crying in the snow on the side of the road left a lasting impression: a shivering boy of just 10 years old, in that moment, I knew I had to take care of my myself and my siblings because our mother couldn't, or wouldn't.

Collecting those cans took a long trek back and forth to the university campus and the recycling center, but I realized quickly that I had other options closer to home. While the other kids my age were playing and goofing off, I taught myself the importance of responsibilities and resilience. I started doing odd jobs around the neighborhood before and after school and it paid a steady couple of dollars every week. Shug caught on fast and told me I needed to start helping to pay for rent and food.

She would leave earlier and come back later and half the time, she'd forget to make us something to eat, leaving us and the fridge behind both half-empty. To pass the time when our mother wasn't home and hopefully distract my brothers and sisters from how hungry they were, I made up a game called Taste Test, where I would line up all of the seasonings and each one of my siblings had to taste each one while I took careful note of their reactions. But they were tired of mushy canned food every night and they got tired of being my guinea pigs quick, and one night they all banded together and decided to stage a hunger strike.

"We want something good!" they squealed, demanding that I fix them something decent. I was only 11 at the time, what could I try to fix besides grilled cheese?

After a few hours with no sign of Shug returning any time soon, I knew that I had to do something. I found the number written down in our phone book to call my Auntie

Dean and standing in the kitchen twirling the phone cord around my fingers, I listened to the ringing and the click and then said, "Hello Auntie, it's me!"

"Terrance Leontha Wallace!" She always called me by my full name. "What are you calling about?"

"We hungry!" I explained the situation to her, tacking on at the end, "Could you please tell me how to make your delicious gravy and chicken?"

I heard laughing through the line but without missing a beat, Auntie Dean asked, "Your mama got some chicken in the refrigerator?" Leaving the phone hanging, I checked the fridge and brought it back, placing it on the counter. She said, "Wash it off."

"With soap?" I asked, teasing her.

She laughed, "No, no!"

I said, "With washing powder?"

Auntie Dean said no again with a big laugh, "Just run it under some water." She told me to sprinkle salt and pepper on it and then asked, "Is there any garlic salt?"

"Yeah!" I said "Yeah, we like that!"

"How you know what it taste like?"

My brothers and sisters crowded around me as they watched their dinner being brought to life, yelled, "He makes us do taste test!"

She told me to put the chicken in the oven at 350° and now was the real test: the gravy. "Put the black pan on the stove and don't turn it up all the way," and then, "Your mama has a grease can on top of the stove."

She instructed me through the phone and I did my best to follow exactly as she said, but the gravy got lumpy all over. Hearing the frustration in my voice, she said patiently, "Don't worry baby, try it again, just like this."

I cleaned and greased the pan again and stirred in the last of the chicken crumb drops. She told me to add water and all of a sudden, the gravy came to life. "*I got it!*" I exclaimed excitedly. At that moment, my brothers and sister's eyes lit up. Each one of them licked the gravy clean off their plates that night.

Auntie Bird heard about it down the grapevine and she ended up telling Shug that I had called long distance to ask how to make the chicken because all the kids were standing around the stove starving to death. She beat me black and blue for sharing our business, but I can still flawlessly make Auntie Dean's gravy from memory.

Half of my siblings work in the restaurant industry today but not all of us picked up a cooking skill set. My sister was expected to cook for the family as the oldest girl. One day Shug called and gave instructions on how to prepare neckbones and tea, so it'd be ready when she got home. She told my sister, "Cut up some onions and tomatoes for the neckbones, boil the neck bones, and boil some tea." On one of the many occasions of retelling this story, Shug would say that when she walked into the house and smelled the neckbones simmering and the tea brewing, she was happy because she felt that my sister was ready to take over the duties in the kitchen. But when she walked in the kitchen, she saw only one pot on the stove.

My sister had done exactly what she was told: our mom didn't tell her to boil the tea and neckbones in separate pots, so the tea, neckbones, tomatoes, and onions were all cooking in together. She's still a terrible cook to this day.

Aunt Dean moved to Detroit with her family because her husband got a job at a car factory, just like Willie Earl. I found out Granddaddy Neal was going to be in the same state as me when I overhead Shug on the phone one day, complaining to one of her friends that her dad hadn't come to visit *her* in Michigan even though she'd been living here for years.

Although Shug had kept me out of contact with my grandparents since she took me away, I seized the opportunity and resolved to write to them, asking for help. In my letter I told them that Shug was taking my money from shoveling snow to fund her Bingo habits and I told them that I had grown up since they last saw me. I promised that I could be of help to them if they would just come and rescue me and take me back home to Alabama with them.

For a week I waited, allowing Shug to beat on me without a peep so that I could be sure that I was home when they came. Instead, I was there when she got mail, shuffling through the bills until she found my letter, her face twisting into a rage as she tore it open and skimmed the page quickly. They never came for me because they never heard my cries for help.

"Dumb fucker can't even send a letter right," she snarled, the letter crumpled in her fist as it rained down on me. I had mixed up the addresses on the envelope and the letter was returned to Shug. "As if you gonna try and share our business and tell somebody what I'm doing up here! Don't you *ever* tell anyone what I been doing!"

What seemed like years of pent-up anger at me never fully accepting her was flowing and as she gave me the whooping of a lifetime, she all but screamed, "I'm not Shug, I'm your mother!"

My classmates liked to hang out at the local arcade and pizza parlor on Saginaw Street, Casanova Go-Go, and even though I spent most afternoons doing yardwork in my neighborhood, it was rare that I had even a few quarters to splurge on some games with them and I didn't want to ask anybody – most of all Shug – for anything.

I asked the owner of the arcade if I could sweep the floor and sidewalk and maybe trim the weeds around the parking lot, too. The owner, a large, friendly man with a round belly and bright red hair, had seemed surprised at my offer, but he took a chance and hired me even though I really wasn't old enough, at just twelve years young.

I worked hard to prove my worth to him, sweeping, washing dishes, and cleaning the arcade. For almost three years, from 5th to 8th grade, I worked there afternoons after school and on the weekends. Eventually they had me taking orders and answering the phone. They taught me how to make the pizzas and sandwiches too. At Casanova Go-Go is where I had my first taste of working in a kitchen, preparing food for people, and experiencing their joy over sharing it together.

If I thought it was bad when I was just shoveling snow, Shug started keeping closer tabs on me, knew my hours and whereabouts and when to hold out her hand for cash from seasonal work or for pay from the arcade and she never showed any semblance of gratitude for my efforts to provide what I could for her or my siblings. We still went to bed hungry most nights.

Eventually, I found a window behind the stove in Casanova Go-Go's kitchen that I would leave open. In secret, I would make extra sandwiches and store them with some sodas in a cooler so I could get them later on for my brothers and sisters and myself. The owner asked me once what I did with my paycheck as he handed it to me and I shrugged and said I was saving the money. Years later, it occurred to me that he knew that my mom was taking the money, and he probably knew about the sandwiches too.

When I was small, Shug liked to use her belt and she liked to throw things, grabbing whatever was closest to her in the heat of the moment and flinging it at me with all she had. Now, as I was getting bigger and stronger, we were more evenly matched and I realized that I could finally stick up for myself. I never got violent back but I would grab whatever she had in her hands and hold it away from her until she was screaming at me to get out.

The times that Shug kicked me out, in the quiet moments when I wasn't in sheer survival mode, I nearly worried myself sick thinking about my brothers and sisters, especially Kory who was just a toddler at the time. Were they crying, were they hungry? I couldn't miss a day of school because that's how I fed myself and checked on them at the playground. After school I would spy on them while doing yardwork for the neighbors, just to make sure they were okay.

One of our neighbors died, an old lady named Miss Johnson who used to pay me to rake the leaves and shovel snow from her driveway. Everybody up and down the street had heard that she died, myself included, and knowing that her house was empty and that I needed a place to sleep, I found an unlocked door in the back and let myself in.

There were no lights and no running water, so I'd have to wash up and take a shower in the changing rooms at school, but nobody bothered me and I kept to myself, relishing the peace and quiet every evening. I stayed there on and off whenever Shug got mad at me for close to 6 months. I was almost 13 then and I had gone through a growth spurt over the summer, so I was about to be taller than her and our tempers were trying to outdo each other more than ever.

I was staying in Miss Johnson's house, but it was the first frosty night of the season and even inside I could see my breath on the air. I lit a fire in the fireplace, just enough to warm up the room. Although I had done such a good job of flying under the radar while I was there and I thought I was being so careful to keep the fire small, a neighbor saw the smoke from the chimney and called Miss Johnson's sons, telling them that someone was squatting in their mama's house.

That same night, even though I hadn't seen them once since her death, her two sons showed up. One came in through the front door and the other through the back and they ambushed me in the living room where I was sleeping in front of the fireplace.

"What do you think you're doing here?" one of the asked me roughly, dragging me out of my sleeping bag in front of the fireplace. I heard the other guy running up the stairs. The first guy squinted at me in the dim light, voice raising to shout up at his brother, "Aw shit, he's just a kid!"

"Everything is there!" was the response that came floating down the stairs, "He didn't touch anything! He didn't take anything!"

It never occurred to me that she might have money or jewelry or anything in her room. I had never even ventured onto the second floor of her home – I had just been relieved for a place to sleep. When the second son came back downstairs, I explained how I had known their mom by taking care of her lawn and driveway and that I was just staying there because I had nowhere else to stay.

Without even talking or discussing it between themselves first, the brothers told me that I could stay until they sold the house, if I would keep shoveling the snow and keep it looking neat and tidy. A week later, they even turned the lights and water on for me and then an envelope started showing up in the mailbox every few weeks with a few dollar bills tucked inside. I was crushed when they told me that the house had finally sold and that I'd have to find somewhere else to stay because I loved living by myself, but I never forgot their kindness.

Uncle Billy came to my school to find me not long after Miss Johnson's house sold. I didn't know that he had moved to Michigan and my first thought was that he had come to take me back to Alabama. Instead, he had heard from Shug that I was living on the streets and she hadn't seen me in a while and so he had come to find me and take me home with him.

At first, I was excited to be staying with Uncle Billy. Single men were granted welfare apartments, a single bed, a sink, and a very small bathroom, and it was cozy. But he stayed with his girlfriend at her place most nights, so I was on my own again. During the first week, there was one can of spam and two cans of corn in the cupboard. I thought my uncle had come to rescue me, that he might come with some food and take care of me, but he didn't return until a week later.

"You left me here with no food!" I yelled at him accusingly and then I begged, "I'm ready to go home to Alabama, please, take me home to Granddaddy and Ma Dear."

"Wrong Foot, you got to learn how to be a man. Mama and Daddy can't take care of you no more." Uncle Bill shook his head and said, "They need help at this point in their life."

I didn't understand at that time because it had been just a few years since I last saw then, but my grandparents had been getting old for a long time and it was catching up. I tried to get him to see that I was bigger now and that I could help. Instead, Uncle Bill said to get dressed. He gave me two dollars and a gas can and told me to go to the gas station and fill up the can.

When I returned, he took me downstairs to an old lawnmower in the shed. Uncle Bill filled her up with the gas I brought back and he pulled and pulled the string until it roared to life. Sparks were flying and black smoke poured from the lawnmower. He looked at me with approval and said, "This the best I can do for you."

I just wanted to be looked after like a regular kid but that day would never come and I've been on the grind my whole life. I had already been looking after myself for months and already had a long list of customers whose lawns I'd been caring for. Once I swallowed my disappointment and started pushing that lawn mower up and down the street, it didn't matter anymore that weeks could go by without me seeing my Uncle Billy. Kids started teasing me at school, saying that I was knocking on everybody's door, begging to cut their grass.

One night, my uncle showed up drunk. Leaning in too close, his words slurring together he said, "Wrong Foot, your pockets look heavy, let me hold onto something for you. I know you got money to buy me a beer."

Ducking out of his way, I shot back, "I ain't got no money for your beer."

Leaning back with a funny expression on his face, he drawled, "Okay then, I can't make no poor hustler out of you." I didn't know what he meant by that, but he said he was going to teach me a lesson. I was happy he never came home that much, because finally, he passed out on the twin bed and I slept on the floor. I soon learned that a fair exchange ain't no robbery.

I got up bright and early the next day to get a jump start on my rounds cutting grass. It was Saturday in Michigan during the summer and people were going to be having yard sales and I thought I might find some good stuff. When I went to get my lawnmower, I found it with a chain hooked to it.

I went upstairs where my uncle was still sleeping, yelling, "Bill, someone chained my lawnmower up!"

Sitting up and rubbing sleep out of his eyes, he said, "I know who did it."

"I got grass to cut!" I exclaimed desperately, "Who!"

With a dry chuckle, he told me, "The owner."

"Who is the owner?" I asked blankly.

"Me!" he explained almost gleefully. "That lawnmower's for sale today at a cheap price."

I spluttered in disbelief. "*What.*" He must have woken up in the middle of the night to do this.

"Yeah, you heard me," he said, "Cheap. Better hurry before the sale expires."

"How much for the lawnmower?" I demanded.

He shot back, "How much you got?"

Outraged, I reached into my pocket and turned my back so he couldn't see how much I had, but he peered nosily over my shoulder. "Damn, Wrong Foot," he said. "I see at least 70 dollars, and I told you I had a cheap price for you today. Give me 30 and that fine machine is all yours."

I gave him the money, cussing him out as I did and he just laughed, "What did I tell you about cussing? I'm your uncle."

I was livid, but I just scowled and I pushed my way past him to finally get the rest of my day started.

"You're a man and you ain't never got to ask nobody for nothing. I showed you how to survive!" Uncle Bill shouted at my back as I slammed the door shut behind me. "You gonna be all right, Wrong Foot, you got your shoes on the right feet now!"

1983-1986: MICHIGAN

The year that I turned 14, Shug finally took me to visit home in Alabama. I was on my best behavior in the months leading up to that summer, terrified that a single misstep might lead to her taking the trip away. "Don't even think for a second about telling them anything," was the only warning she gave me on the long drive down, giving me a hard stare through the rearview mirror.

The first weeks we were there, it felt like I had all the time in the world, like the summer would stretch on for an eternity. I may have protested loudly at being smothered in hugs and kisses by Ma Dear and Tha-Boo, squirming and wriggling the whole time, but secretly I was overjoyed to be doted on again. They cooked me everything I loved the most and for the first time in years I ate second and third and fourth helpings of dinner, my grandmothers piling another portion onto my plate before the first was even done. And even though three years had passed, we were still just kids and fitting in again with my cousins and friends was effortless, like nothing had changed at all.

I was sure they must have heard something from Uncle Billy, who I stayed with on and off when Shug kicked me out, but I dodged any questions about life in Michigan with superficial, non-specific answers that seemed to satisfy them. For weeks, I didn't even think about the hardships I would have to face when we returned to Michigan, but the summer began to draw to an end. Ma Dear flipped the page of the calendar hanging on the kitchen wall and the date of our departure, circled in thick red marker, loomed aggressively at me until it was the only thing I could think about.

It was easy falling back into old and comforting routines and I had spent most weekends with Jimmy and Tha-Boo. But, overwhelmed with anxiety from the thought of leaving, I snapped the next time I saw Jimmy. Words I had promised Shug not to say tumbled over themselves in a rush to leave my mouth, explaining what had been happening to me since I was taken away – her anger and her violence, how she would kick me out from time to time, how hungry I was more often than not, how badly I wanted to *stay*.

"I'll get to the bottom of this," Jimmy reassured me with a firm squeeze when I finally fell silent, "You don't have to go anywhere."

Shug called Granddaddy Neal's house a few hours after I returned and as soon as the phone was put in my hand, I knew she was pissed. *"Boy!"* she yelled, voice shrill and staticky through the line. "You tell me why Jimmy gonna have the *nerve* to call me up and interrogate me about what I do and don't do in the privacy of my own home!"

I hadn't even opened my mouth to defend myself before her next words tauntingly shattered what remained of my old life: "He can't *save* you - he ain't even your real daddy."

I don't remember the details of how the rest of that conversation went, but Shug told me to go to the corner store because someone was there that I had to meet. I don't remember actually going there either, but I know I sat on the bench outside of it for a little while trying to gather myself. A man came out of the store and stood in front of me, blocking the sun.

It was only silent for a moment and I was about to ask him who he was, before a woman walking past us said, "Sam! He look just like you. Is that your son?" as she went into the store.

"Hello Terry, how are you?" the man said to me in a friendly voice when the door to the store had closed behind her. "My name is Sam and I'm your father."

Ma Dear and even Granddaddy Neal tried to ask me what was wrong when I came home that night but I didn't know how to tell them what I had learned, so I clammed up. The truth confused and consumed me and I was in a daze for the remainder of my time in Alabama. Everything passed around me in a blur as I struggled to process the discovery of my biological father's identity.

I knew kids who had no idea who their dads were, I just never thought it would be an issue for *me*. I didn't want to believe in yet another new and harsh reality that Shug had once again forced upon me. In my mind, I examined my childhood, searching for a clue of my lifelong deceit. At the time, it felt like everyone I had ever known was lying to me. Angry and hurt, I did my best to shut them all out.

It would take me years to put all the pieces together and fully understand the implications of Shug's deceit. I would find out that she was 15 years old when she got pregnant with me – just a few years older than I was when I found out – and that she had been messing around with two boys who both could've been the daddy. Sam had a baby with another girl already and Jimmy didn't and so, to Shug, it was a logical decision. Her two boyfriends were a poorly kept secret, but Jimmy accepted me wholeheartedly, never once doubting her intentions or me. As I got older, I would lie awake late at night, imagining how Tha-Boo and Ma Dear must have silently endured all the looks, the stares, the whispers of speculation that floated on the air as they held my hand as we walked through the neighborhood.

But back then, when Jimmy came to pick me up to spend our last weekend of the summer together, I couldn't bring myself to face him or Tha-Boo with this new-found knowledge. I hid in the woods for hours and I didn't return until it was late and I was sure that he had driven back to the city. Back then, I didn't know if they knew the truth and it felt like it was my responsibility to break their hearts by telling them.

Shug came to pick me up to go back to Michigan right before the leaves on the trees changed from green to orange and I found that I was relieved to get into her car. I had refused to see Jimmy and Tha-Boo since I found out. I couldn't bear to look them in the eyes knowing about this manipulation. The shame I carried for her mistreatment of people that I loved so dearly made me distance myself and it would be a long time before I saw them again. When I left childhood behind and grew into a man – even though my face looked nothing like his – we never talked about the truth. Jimmy never had another kid and he always referred to me as his son.

The year after returning from Alabama, I threw myself into all the work I could find, determined to forget the truth I had learned. I was good enough that I could have been on the football or basketball team at school but uniforms and gear were expensive, and besides that, I didn't have the time to commit to practice and games since I was too busy working and paying bills and rent and buying and stealing food to feed myself and my siblings. It just seemed no matter what I gave it was never enough.

My nickname came to be Four Seasons, because when I wasn't at school or working at Casanova Go-Go, I had a rake in my hand for leaves in the fall, a shovel for snow in the winter, and a lawn mower for grass in the spring and summer.

I was 15 years old and the air was heavy with the humidity of late August and earlier that day, some of my hard-earned money had been used to buy me new clothes for school, since I was still growing like a weed and nothing fit right. Shug turned and said to me, "You got your clothes. Now what are you going to do about your brothers and sisters?" All four of them couldn't use my hand-me-downs at the same time. She wailed that Willie Earl never did anything for them besides drag us to Michigan and smoke away their money.

Although she never directly told me to steal, Shug was a master of manipulation and the way she presented her situation messed with me deep down in my psyche. Shug planted the seed and I did what I thought was necessary to care for my brothers and sisters and gain her love and approval. I had seen them hide the cash register in the space under the stairs while working the closing shift at Casanova Go-Go. That night, I shimmied in through the window I left open to retrieve the sandwiches I had hidden earlier during my shift. I didn't even take more than twenty or thirty dollars, but I sprinted all the way home, my heartbeat pounding in my ears. I forgot to take the sandwiches.

Banging on the front door and then loud voices in the hall announced that I had been busted and that the police were looking for me. They took me back to the scene of the crime and I had to face the owner with equal feelings of shame and regret coursing through me. With time, I would become numb to any of those feelings. The owner of Casanova Go-Go had been nothing but good to me but this was a matter of survival, for myself and my family. He chose not to press charges on me but all of the trust I had built with them had been destroyed and he told me not to bother coming back.

The police returned me home to Shug and she never mentioned it once.

Once I had lost my job at the pizza place, I made do for a little while by doubling my yardwork efforts. But I had holes in my shoes and a friend told me to come with him one day late in the afternoon, saying, "I'm gonna get you a job with my brother."

He brought me to a place I had walked by thousands of times but never once until that day had I even lingered or considered going inside. It was an unkept house with burglar bars around the windows and doors and dark inside from heavy drawn curtains and dim, tungsten lightbulbs casting endless shadows.

First, I started selling weed to kids at my school. Then they promoted me and I manned the door at the drug house from 11 o'clock at night until the sun had started rising at 7 the following morning. They would lock us inside the house and desperate addicts would come knocking on the door, asking for a fix. We'd pass them dime bags with small rocks inside that somebody else had packaged up, taking 5, 10, 20 dollars in exchange.

I was just fifteen at the time and even though I had started working out I was still lanky and all elbows and knees. I wasn't even shaving yet. My days were a haphazard routine of skipping morning classes and showing up to school to eat lunch, maybe staying for the afternoon, maybe not. I would spend my afternoons doing yardwork around the neighborhood. If I wasn't couch surfing because Shug had kicked me out again, I'd sneak out at 11 for my shift at the drug house and then come back in the morning before she got up. Often, when I was homeless, I'd just crash on a dingy mattress on the floor of one of the rooms.

The first few times I was scared, mind still filled with all the things I'd heard teachers and supposed figures of authority preaching during assemblies at school. But after each shift, we'd get fifty bucks cash in hand to go home with and the money spoke louder than they ever did.

I landed an opportunity to work in the cafeteria at Harry Hill Vocational School through the Summer Youth Job Program. My only problem was that I needed a work permit. I was staying between my friend's houses and my uncle's apartment because I was in and out of Shug's house – more *out* than *in*, really: staying at her house was conditional and depended entirely on my willingness to submit to her and surrender my money. When I didn't, she would put me out. Going to her to get the paper signed was not an option for me. I didn't dare ask her because if she knew that I had another source of income, she would put more pressure on me and take what little money I had left.

I got my best friend to forge my mother's signature on the slip. This was my first real job, with taxes taken off my paycheck and I stopped working nights at the drug house. I started doing general kitchen work at first, cleaning, mopping, sweeping, dishes, and setting up tables and chairs in the dining areas. Eventually they let me handle money and work the register. But the kitchen in the vocational school cafeteria was unlike anything I had ever seen before – compared to the pizza joint, walking into this industrial kitchen was like walking into NASA.

Being in there, in close proximity to that kitchen with shiny new stainless-steel machinery and gadgets – the ovens and stovetops and grill, the fryer, and the flattop – I felt like a kid in a candy store. I wanted to know how everything worked. It lit a fire under me and I was hungry to learn. In no time I was asking my supervisors if there wasn't anything more that I could do. Then they started training me in basic prep work, and then as a line cook, preparing meals for the teachers' lounge and the students in the cafeteria.

But I had skipped so much schooling during the last year that it was inevitable that they would kick me out. I wasn't allowed back when classes started up again after the summer. "I have a job!" I protested at the meeting with my guidance counsellor.

"You can't go to regular high school if you have to keep a job," she explained to me, understanding and sympathetic. "But you can go to adult education – you'll get credits towards a diploma for vocational training." That woman was heaven sent, truly an angel, because I kept my job and I kept getting paid, and I was still getting an education. In the morning, I would do the vocational program and then in the afternoon, I had a job to do through the work program. After 2 years, when I was 17, I graduated with my first culinary degree: a food-handlers certification.

The summer that I got my driver's license, I started saving money to buy a car. I paid rent to Shug when I was there, bought clothes for my sisters and brothers, and I still managed to save up enough money to buy my first set of wheels from the owner of Dennis Distributing. They were in the business of selling household appliances but the owner had a Chevy Chevette for sale in the parking lot for five hundred dollars.

About two weeks after I bought the car, the clutch went out. I spoke to Shug's friend on the phone about the car and he told me how to file a small claim in court. She overheard our conversation and before I could take action, she took that information down to Dennis Distributing to advocate for me – at least that's how she presented herself afterwards. It's easier to ask for forgiveness than permission.

Shug used her status as my mother and legal guardian to talk the owner into taking my car back in exchange for a new washer and dryer. When the deal was done, she handed me the refund of fifty dollars. All summer, I had worked two jobs and hustled for my siblings and myself. All I had to show for it was a single fifty-dollar bill.

Over the next year, I saved up again and bought another car. Shug's relationship with Willie Earl was deteriorating and they had split up again. She got herself a job as a substitute teacher at a nearby middle school, finally using her degree for the first time since she had gotten it.

I would have been proud of her but I hadn't even been driving myself to school in my new car for two weeks when she took my keys and told me, "Terry! I have a job teaching now – I need your car to go to work." When I graduated, I was still taking walking and taking the bus everywhere.

For a few years, I had managed to keep my head down and stay out of any serious trouble, but I was the man of the house at this point, working a summer job and a night job, alongside my vocational studies. It was rare that Willie Earl was around and when he did show up, Shug would act a fool, screaming and cursing him out at the top of her lungs.

My brothers and sisters were growing faster than I could keep up with and in constant need of clothes. I was already sacrificing every spare moment I had to make sure they got what they needed. The summer after I graduated, I was 17 and my friends were talking about breaking into the Adidas warehouse. Initially, it wasn't something I wanted to be a part of, but they egged me on and I caught on quick, realizing that this was an opportunity to get gear for my siblings that was actually cool and wouldn't get them picked on at school. Covertly, I looked inside my siblings' shoes and clothes and on a scrap of paper I made a list with their names and sizes.

My friends and I were quieter than we had ever been as we prowled the streets of Lansing until the late hours of the night, waiting for our chance. The area was made up of factories and warehouses and Adidas had rented some of it for storage space. Anticipation bubbled and I was nervous and anxious and alert. We were all still so young, most of us only just past high school and really, we had no business being out and about this late.

We broke in through a window and inside of the warehouse, the rest of our group were like wild animals, grabbing at anything they could reach. Whether it was for themselves or to flip later on for a profit, they didn't care either way. I was on the hunt, more selective and efficient because I was doing it for a reason, searching for specific sizes on the boxes and looking for things that I thought my siblings would like. I was reaching for a box marked with the sizes I needed when I tripped the alarm.

We hauled ass out of the warehouse, headed for the car, and for a brief, glorious moment, it felt like we would get away with it. Then out of nowhere, we were surrounded, and one of the police officers responding to the alarm grabbed me and slammed me down as hard as he could on the concrete, knocking the wind right out of my lungs.

He kicked roughly at me, turning me over with his foot and in the same moment, he seemed to realize both how young I was and just how hard he struck me. Sprawled out on my back looking up at him – a rigid military type guy with skin dark like mine – my head was spinning, eyes glassy and watering and I struggled and gasped for air. "Breathe, kid…breathe!" the cop said, a little calmer.

More than once I have been flooded with gratitude to that cop for my life. Just over three decades later, I watched the video of Earl Floyd's death – an eight-minute long video that a bystander caught of white police officers kneeling on the neck of a black man until his last words were, *"I can't breathe."* Similar stories had been coming to light for years but that video sparked a racial justice movement and nationwide protests against systemic racism and police brutality in the weeks that followed, unseen since the civil rights movement of the sixties.

"What do you have in your hand?" he asked me sharply, ordering me to drop it. The list that I had written with my sisters and brothers' names and sizes was still tightly grasped in my fist as I lay on the concrete, winded and shocked at getting caught.

In the moment, panicking and still trying to breathe, I couldn't comprehend his question or command to drop the scrap of paper. He grabbed it from my hand and saw that it was a list.

"You're taking orders, huh?" the officer accused.

"No, sir!" I finally managed to find my breath and gasped out, "It's for my brothers and sisters."

The officer's face changed, his entire demeanor and disposition softening in that moment. He pulled me up and cuffed me and said to me in a low voice, almost regretfully, as he loaded me into the back of his car, "I wish I could let you go, but I can't."

That night, my friends and I went to jail and we stayed there, locked up, for two days. On the second day, we went before the judge and I watched as my friend's moms all came to court to be present for their sons. Shug didn't bother to show up.

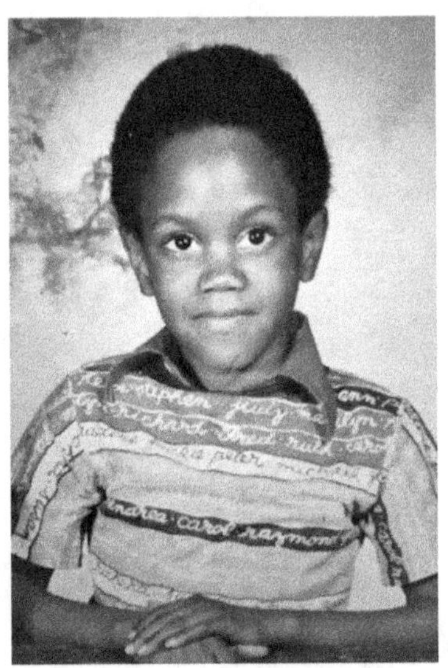

Chef Tee, age 6,
Birmingham, AL

Chef Tee, age 12

2003 with my childhood friend
Fox (on the left)

2006, Grand Rapids, MI
First week out of prison,
Chef Tee to the right

Before Prison

1986-1989: MICHIGAN

After I graduated from the vocational school and had put the Adidas warehouse incident behind me, I got myself another job. Catching the bus and long walks to and from work had become the norm for me because Shug was still using my car. Walking and taking the bus suited me fine, as long as I could still get around and even when I had the graveyard shift, usually I was lucky and could get a friend to give me a ride. But one night, it was going to be late when I got off. The busses wouldn't be running at that hour and everyone I knew was busy.

As much as I didn't want to, I used the office phone to call Shug and ask if she could pick me up. In response, she snapped that I was a grown man and that I needed to find my own way home the best way that I could. I was tired after a long ass shift and didn't even have the energy to snap back that she was driving wheels that I paid for, and I ended the call.

James, this kid that I worked with, overheard me on the phone and told me he had already offered someone else a ride home and that he was headed in the same direction. We'd never even really talked like that during our shifts together but he'd always struck me as nice, and gratefully, I accepted his offer. He towered over most everyone and his car was comedically small. Even though I've never been considered short, out of the three of us, I was the smallest and the other guy called shotgun, so I folded myself into the backseat. We must have looked like clowns squeezing ourselves into a clown car at the circus.

It started off like any other drive: the air conditioning was broken so we drove with the windows down, listening to the radio and talking shit and complaining about our manager. Not long after we had hit the road, we were idling at a red light when a car pulled up in the lane beside us. The driver started revving their engine, shouting and dissing James' tiny car through their open window into ours, trying to goad him into a race. I didn't even know that much about cars back then but I knew that James didn't stand a chance, and I found out that he was as hot headed as he was stupid.

When the light shifted red to orange to green, James mashed his foot to the gas pedal, and both cars took off with a screech. I hoped initially that they'd just go the short stretch between lights but they kept racing faster and faster and I realized that James had no intention of admitting defeat. We ran a red light and then I remembered the way that the road curved up ahead and from the backseat, I was screaming over their laughter, begging for him to stop, to slow down, anything. Then the steering wheel twisted in his hands as he attempted to straighten out the swerving car and James lost control, sending us straight into a pole.

I woke up around four days later and my mind was foggy and my body sore as hell. Vaguely, I remembered voices shouting and the bright white lights of an operating room. My arm and head were wrapped in bandages and gingerly, I started assessing the damage. My head was pounding and as I continued to feel around, I felt more bandages and stitches.

Later on, when they realized I was awake, a doctor told me that I was thrown out of the rear window on impact because I wasn't wearing a seatbelt. When I was located, I was 15 feet away from the car, bleeding from my head and unconscious. I had basically been scalped and my Jheri curl was ruined, adding more scars to the top of my head. My finger was almost severed off completely and a chunk of meat was torn from my shoulder. The doctor explained that if I hadn't landed on my shoulder first, it was likely that I would have broken my neck.

James and the other kid in the car walked away from the accident without even a scratch. I was fired from that job because I stopped showing up for work since I was in the hospital and they never came to check on how I was doing and I never saw them again.

After a month and a half in the hospital, the doctors released me to spend the rest of my recovery at home. This time, when I called to ask for a ride, Shug was more than willing to come and pick me up – to this day, the irony still tastes a little bitter. She showed up and brought me a sweet new pair of Jordan's that she paid for with money that I didn't have to work to give her and for a few moments I indulged myself, allowing myself to believe that she was showing some real concern because I was her son who had almost lost my life. I wanted her to love me so desperately.

This was the longest I had ever been unable to work and without a job since I was literally ten years old and relying on her so completely again made me feel like a child again. She drove me home in a car I hadn't seen before that still had the price spray painted on the windows and I wondered if she had turned her life around while I was in the hospital. I didn't even ask her what she did with my car.

During that time, Shug had officially separated from Willie Earl after seven years of marriage. He was already seeing someone else and she had shifted her attention to a new guy who would come and pull up to our house like a pimp. He was a cool slickster type who wore thick and thin socks and had a different suit for each day of the week. My siblings and I wondered to each other what he would wear in the heat of the summer and when it rolled around that year, we saw that the pants turned into shorts and he wore the vest with no shirt under it.

Shug had gotten herself out of a toxic marriage but the thing about her choice in men was that they were always deeply questionable. Just like Willie Earl, her new man had another woman on the side. During the time that they were together, if he wasn't at the house, taking up space and eating our food, she was away from home battling for his affection. I, not so silently, believed that – just like her last man – his motive was to slick her out of her welfare check.

Late one afternoon the phone started ringing and as though by divine intervention, I happened to be home alone. It was a representative from the insurance company and it turned out that she was looking for *me*. My mother had been hustling her by requesting insurance money on my behalf as my legal guardian, with neither my knowledge nor my consent, but the insurance lady recognized her game.

I had let myself believe that she was taking such good care of me just because she cared – but of course there was money in it for her. In just a handful of months I would become a legal adult and we agreed that Shug wasn't going to see another penny. I would receive the remaining insurance payout of twenty-five thousand dollars upon my 18th birthday. When Shug found out that I had gone over her head and cut her out, we had a huge blow up and that same afternoon, I packed a bag and left before she could kick me out again.

I stayed nearby at first, going to some friends until I could get to Detroit to stay with Aunt Dean. For nearly half a year I lived there and when I finally turned 18, I got a check for $25,000 dollars from the insurance company. I felt giddy holding that piece of paper, nervous I would somehow lose it on my way to deposit it in the bank and the seven days it took for the check to clear were unbearable.

The money got me an apartment that was just across the street from Shug's house. My new place was on the third floor and from the kitchen window I could see her driveway and keep an eye on my brothers and sisters, undetected. I had cut ties with her and we hadn't spoken since the day the insurance people called, but I was still committed to looking out for my siblings and made sure to see them as much as I could.

Before I even bought furniture for my place, I took my brothers and sisters shopping for new clothes. The very next day, they showed up at my place and told me that our mother had taken their bags of new things right out of their hands and gone to get refunds and walk away with the cash. As soon as I heard, we went right back to the mall and bought all of the clothes again and this time I made sure that I took the tags off and kept the receipts.

But in spite of all the bad blood, I still had a soft spot for Shug as the woman who brought me into this world. I pulled Red to the side and stuffed a wad of thirty Benjamins folded securely in her pocket and I sent them home to Shug with three thousand dollars.

Shug interrogated them and eventually found out where I was living and at first, she was enraged that I was so close. From time to time, she would come banging on my door – not to see me, but to demand money. I recognized the rhythm of her knocks, could see her silhouetted through the peephole. Instead of answering I would ignore her and audibly check the locks, pulling the chain latch back and forth a few times for good measure until she got the message and went away. For three years, I lived in that apartment and for all three of those years, I refused to see her.

Between the insurance money and workman's comp, I was comfortable for about a year. At this point, some of my boys had moved in with me and there were five of us staying in that one-bedroom apartment. My friends – Jimbo, Corky, Ivory, and Woochie – were all kids from my neighborhood block, cut from the same cloth of single mothers and absent fathers. For the first time in all of our lives, we had a place to stay where we didn't have to worry about getting kicked out. But my account started to run low and I needed to find a new source of income. Woochie came at us with a get-rich quick plan of learning how to sell crack.

Until then, we had all worked paycheck-to-paycheck at minimum wage jobs, struggling to make ends meet. We were all driven by hunger for more than just surviving, and the way that Woochie pitched the idea, turning the opportunity down seemed crazier than the risk of actually doing it – and if we didn't do it, somebody else would. Woochie had the hook up and together, the five of us learned the science behind the hustle.

In the early 80's, cocaine was a white man's drug, glamorized by movies like Scarface and used by the social elite, inaccessible and unaffordable to lower income communities. Moving drugs like that meant you were a middleman for someone else who had more money and power than you. But freebasing cocaine gave a new method of consuming the drug that almost eliminated the middleman completely. A little science goes a long way and with some careful measuring and mixing, you could take an investment of a couple hundred bucks of cocaine and cook it into smokable crack rocks to flip for an unhealthy profit.

Before we even considering getting involved, the government was already cracking down on crack, spending millions to fund the War on Drugs, with the media whipping the public into a frenzy about crackheads. I had seen the tiny glass vials with crystal rocks, watched transactions go down in hushed voices when I was selling weed at the drug house, but this was the first time the opportunity had presented itself to me so plainly.

We handled the entire supply chain, cooking it and packaging it up, selling the little vials for five or ten bucks a hit. Cooking was second nature to me and it was easy to adapt the skills I'd learned in the kitchen to play this game with success.

Early on around the time I started hustling, Willie Earl started popping up on me more and more, telling me that he heard that I was selling drugs, asking if I had any on me, making a theatrical fatherly attempt to scold me as though him and Shug were still shacked up. It was all just a show. He never bothered trying to be father to me and we had never been anything that resembled close in all those years he was married to my mother. Looking back on my childhood, it's easy to recognize that Willie Earl was a crackhead, disappearing for days on end or strung out and manic the times he was home.

Willie Earl heard from somebody he knew who we were selling to, that we were cooking up some good shit and he wanted a taste. He approached me once on the sidewalk outside my apartment and he asked me if I wanted his help to make some money. This was the first time in our entire relationship that he had offered me his help. "Come by my place tonight," he told me, "And make sure you bring some weight."

We didn't need his help but we were greedy: crackheads popped up like weeds and our biggest problem was that we couldn't seem to supply enough to keep up with demand. As much as I just wanted to flex on him and show him how far I had risen, I started dealing with Willie

Earl again out of a lack of – or maybe even more, a desire for – a paternal figure.

Woochie came with me to make the deal and we packed more than we thought they would buy from us. "How much you need?" I questioned, making myself comfortable in an armchair in the living room, my backpack on the floor between my feet. Woochie sat on the adjacent couch and there were a handful of Willie Earl's friends in the house, all people I recognized from around the block.

"How much you got?" Willie Earl asked with a skewed eyebrow and a crooked grin. They bought everything we had. We were in and out in less than fifteen minutes, having sold the equivalent of what we would've after standing for hours on the corner. Whatever mixed feelings I'd had about dealing with Willie Earl disappeared as I counted the stack of bills back at home. It was such a smooth and easy payoff that they quickly become some of our most important customers and we would stop by and do deals whenever he called.

There is a certain type of safety in numbers and usually one of my boys came with me, but it was inevitable that I would end up going there by myself. It was easy to get comfortable in Willie Earl's living room, making small talk and drinking a cold can of soda as we made the deal. The zipper on my backpack signaled my departure and as I stood to leave, Willie Earl leaned over and told me to stick around for a while.

I wasn't naive as to what happened after I left, I just preferred not to think about it. I could cook it up but once it left my hands it was no longer my business. It was easier not to think about the side effects my hustle had on the community around me – it was a simple transaction, crack was just a rock that equaled money and I needed that money to survive.

"So, it's true then," Willie Earl tapped one of the vials I had given him against a small glass pipe to drop the crystals into it and handed it to me. "Don't get high on your own supply," he said, making air quotes around his words with his fingers. "You really never had a taste?"

I shook my head, eyeing the pipe in my hand warily. I had never seen anyone using the drugs I gave them, let alone had interest in wanting to try them myself. "Never."

He barked out a laugh and reached out and took the pipe back from me. "How's a chef supposed to send out a dish he ain't even tasted?"

I shrugged, but his friends, watching our interaction from spots around the room, laughed with him. Willie Earl held the pipe up to his lips with one hand, thumb flicking the lighter in the other, holding the flame under the pipe. When heated, crack makes a popping sound, snapping and crackling as it melts – ergo its name. He inhaled deeply, pulling the smoke into his lungs and I couldn't help but watch curiously as he held it in for a moment and then sagged back into the couch behind him, exhaling slowly.

"Whoo-ee!" he whistled through his teeth, foot bouncing restlessly on the rug. His eyes were lidded as though he struggled to keep them open. "That's the stuff! Make you feel on top of the world and shit." He laughed and whooped again, louder this time. "You know your shit sonny boy! How you know this ain't for you?"

Suddenly, I wasn't so sure. He seemed jittery, spaced out, but this didn't look like the crackhead picture painted by the media. Making a getaway before it got this far was easy, but when the vibe was like this, with the smell of weed hanging heavy in the air and music and murmuring in the background, saying no was so much harder. "I don't," I mused, leaning forward in my seat and turning the thought over in my brain. "Maybe just a little taste."

Willie Earl shifted excitedly, bouncing like a child. He re-upped the pipe with another hit, passing it back to me with the lighter. It was small in my hand and I looked down at it for a moment, trying to not lose my nerve. I didn't want to look like a pussy.

I tried to steady my hand as I raised it to my lips and I fumbled with the lighter a few times before the flame caught. I sucked the smoke in like a fish out of water and could barely hold it for a moment before I was spluttering and coughing. But the rush was instantaneous and intoxicating, this sense of euphoria hitting me like a truck. I couldn't even speak for a minute, basking in momentary bliss. "Oh man," I said finally and again, everyone in the

room laughed, but it felt different this time because now –
I was in on the secret. "Oh *man*."

The high didn't last more than 15 minutes. I don't
remember what was said as I left and my feet felt like bricks
as I made my way down the driveway to my car. My heart
was racing, and my hands were trembling so hard it took
me a few tries to get the engine running. I sat in the car
for a while, hands clutching the wheel as I stared blankly
ahead of me. I had been worried throughout my recovery
from the accident that I'd get hooked on the painkillers
the doctors were prescribing me. Turns out it was my ex-
stepfather I needed to be afraid of.

Our main stomping ground was the same vocational
school that I graduated from. We were supplying the entire
adult education with drugs. The come up was almost
instantaneous and we went from just barely scraping
by to pulling in stacks of cash. Now we were living like
young kings and our everyday became one endless party,
suddenly with disposable income to spend on women and
clothes and a good time. I bought a Nissan 200z to replace
the cars that Shug had claimed from me as a teenager.
I decked it out with shiny rims and tinted windows and
huge speakers that made the ground underneath the car
shake when the music was blasting. My car was the envy
of the block and the kid who ran after the bus became the
man.

But I wasn't the only one who started occasionally sampling our own product and the rest of my crew picked up drug habits along the way. As fun and exciting as it all felt in the beginning, that environment was deadly. At first it was an adrenaline rush and then it became a nightmare, making you paranoid like you couldn't trust anybody. Drugs are non-discriminating: they don't care who you are, what you do, what you look like…they are powerfully mind altering and if you want to go right, the drugs tell you to go left.

I saw girls in the high school bathroom trading sex for drugs, beautiful girls who could've been super models throwing their lives away and turning into mindless mummies. We needed guns to protect ourselves from rival dealers trying to get in on our turf and I have more than one friend who put their lives on the line and died for what we believed was a worthy cause.

Back then, there was no time to be affected by the horrific reality we had created for ourselves — it was a matter of survival, simply making it through one day to rinse and repeat again the next.

By the end of the 80's and the start of the 90's, the War on Drugs had engulfed the entire nation and we were fighting a losing battle against crack as it decimated our communities. Billions of dollars were spent on law enforcement and the expansion of the prison system which led to an exploding number of incarcerations. In a national address, President Bush senior held up a bag of crack rocks supposedly bought across the street from the White House and said to the population of America, "It's as innocent looking as candy but it's turning our nation into battle zones."

We had been moving some serious weight and a Federal Drug Charge was started in Michigan. I had been driving back and forth to Detroit, up and down the highway, picking up kilos to bring back to Lansing and there was a solid chance my name would be on the indictment list for transportation and conspiracy. Some of the guys I was dealing with were getting serious time and I was scared they would snitch on me.

The Anti-Drug Abuse Act mandated possession of 5 grams of crack punishable by a minimum sentence of 5 years – mandating the same sentence for 500 grams of cocaine, a 1:100 disparity. I was barely a legal adult, less concerned with how my decision to hustle affected everyone else around me and more worried about saving my own ass, so I fled the state, taking refuge down south with my family in Alabama.

1989-1993: ALABAMA

I went into panic mode and sold everything I owned and I snuck out of town late one night on a Greyhound bus bound south. It was early fall when I left and the leaves on the trees were just beginning to shift from green to red and orange and gold. I left Michigan the same way I had come: with nothing but the clothes on my back, the shoes on my feet, and a backpack stuffed with my most important possessions. The difference was that this time, I was in control of where I was going, and why.

It's easier to ask for forgiveness than permission, so I didn't give anyone a heads up of my homecoming. I had been gone for too long and I didn't know what to say to them over the phone. Instead, I knocking on Auntie Bobbie's front door, showing up tired and disheveled after days on the road. She was the polar opposite of her sister Shug – a quiet, church going woman who was sweet like molasses and never had a bad thing to say about anyone – and had always talked to me like an adult, even when I was a child. Her and her husband, Uncle Boot, opened their home to me and let me stay with them, without question.

They lived in a three-bedroom apartment and all in all, we were six people living there. There really wasn't space for me and I slept in the living room on the floor, but besides the occasional spat, they never said a negative

"

thing against me. It took time for me to refamiliarize myself with my family, people who I had once known and loved like the back of my own hand but now felt more like strangers.

Auntie Bobbie lived and died by her church. They only had 15 members as long as I could remember and most of them were in their late 70's. That included the whole congregation. The reverend was the choir director, guitar player, drummer, and tambourine player. That nigga would put on a show screaming, hollering, and yelling for two hours straight. My cousin Sam and I would go with her and we'd barely be able to make eye contact, or we'd be cracking up the whole time.

Uncle Boot used to raise hell about Auntie Bobbie paying tithe at church, saying during dinner every Sunday night, "Woman, you willing to give that goddam preacher all our damn money! They been promising a new parking lot for the last three years but all I see is that preacher with a new car in the same old parking lot!" He was ready to give anyone the business. He gave the preacher the business once.

One Sunday after church, Auntie Bobbie invited the preacher over for lunch, which Uncle Boot felt strongly about, because that was during his drinking time. He would sit on the porch almost non-stop as soon as he got home from work Friday night to Sunday night, drinking beers and shooting the shit with the neighbors and then back to work Monday through Friday.

My cousins and uncle and I were drinking on the porch, beer cans scattered all over, when Auntie Bobbie pulled up. "Get this shit off my porch," she said announcing her plans for lunch sweetly in her church voice, making us double over in laughter. "Who's funding this party anyway?" She controlled the finances in their household and she wondered who funded this drinking party on a Sunday.

I raised my hand with a tipsy grin and she slapped me lightly across the head on her way inside and said again, "Clean this shit up! I'm serving lunch on the porch."

Uncle Boot cussed under his breath about the party being put on hold and grumbled, "This my goddam house…" as he chugged the last of his beer and instructed my cousin and I. "Help each other bring the table out here."

The preacher arrived a few hours later and when we were all seated at the table, Uncle Boot gestured his head admiringly at his car parked out front and said, "The church must be paying you pretty good."

"Hey there," the preacher turned his hands outward as though to ask God himself, "We still need some help with parking lot!" Auntie Bobby was fixing everyone a plate and moved to give the preacher a chicken leg and thigh. He quickly covered his plate with his hand and with a big smile on his face said, "I don't eat dark meat, only white, thank you."

"You don't eat dark meat," Uncle Boot repeated flatly, his eyes cutting left and we all knew what was coming. Even Auntie Bobbie knew what time it was.

The preacher replied, "No, sir, cheapest part of the chicken!"

"So, first you gonna slick-talk my wife out of all our money at that church of yours and then you gonna come to my house, and negro, you too good for to eat dark meat?" Uncle Boot's voice boomed, fists pounding the table as he rose to his feet. "Get your goddam ass outta my house."

Despite my unwillingness to face up to the consequences of my actions in Michigan, when I returned to Alabama, I saw a gap in the market and my instincts told me to risk it all again and get back in the game, hard. Even though I had moved across the country, I was still connected with all the right people in that world. Hustlers in the Detroit area, like myself, used more advanced marketing techniques to secure their customers than they had seen down South yet: Double Ups were a 2-for-1 deal on crack rocks and when I brought Double Ups with me, in one fell swoop I was yet again making a killing for myself and literally killing the community around me – the community that raised me when I was a child.

I respected Auntie Bobbie enough that I made a private pact with myself to never sell any drugs from her home.

I had no space of my own, so I got two jobs to try to reestablish myself and stayed at work as much as I could. I felt as though I was taking measures to keep her home and family protected and set what I thought were firm boundaries. I was careful to always meet my customers in discreet meeting spots around town, but where I was staying wasn't a secret and when a person who has an addiction wants to get high, they lose all discretion and boundaries are crossed.

One day while I wasn't at home, a scrawny, shifty looking dude came knocking on my Auntie's door looking for a fix. He asked my Auntie if she had a dime and knowing absolutely nothing about drugs or their lingo, she naïvely left him standing at the door and told him to hold on so that she could get her coin purse. God bless her heart, my Auntie thought she was just trying to be helpful and returned to the stranger standing before her and she handed him a shiny dime.

In disappointment, the dude said, "I'm here for the drugs…I need the dope!" The look on her face was probably one of grim shock and sometimes I wish I had been there to witness her shooing him off her porch. Auntie Bobbie had probably been hearing rumors about me around town but I never once heard her gossiping about anyone, and most likely she had chosen not to believe them. That visit to her front door let her know that something was going on.

It was her son, my cousin, who ended up confirming her fears later that day. In the moment, I had been livid that he had ratted me out, but with time I would come to understand. When we were little, growing up together, me and him were more like brothers but when I was relocated to Michigan, I had to hustle in a way he never did. I was different when I came back and he was timid in how he carried himself as he observed how I moved.

My auntie and I talked for hours. I hadn't told them why I decided to come back now, but I knew that they occasionally spoke to Shug. I also hadn't told her the exact reason for my departure, but I was sure she had heard some gossip down the grapevine.

I was not the same Terry that they had known before I was taken from my grandparents and dragged to Michigan and I finally all that I had been going through since Shug and Willie Earl took me from Alabama spilled out: the responsibility of working and providing for and raising my siblings, Shug taking my money, the car accident, the beatings, cooking and dealing crack. Auntie Bobbie made me go to the closet and take it all out: the drugs, the money, the guns I had for handling any possible physical altercations and for protecting myself. My auntie held my hand and she cried and cried and she told me that she didn't want to watch me die.

Auntie Bobbie had shown me the first true motherly concern that I had felt in close to a decade and for the first time, I was motivated to get my life back on the straight and narrow. Although generally, I ate my meals away from home because I didn't want to take up space at the apartment, I cooked once or twice for Auntie Bobbie and rediscovered my love for the kitchen. I walked into probably fifteen different spots before I passed by the Wall Street Deli, a small deli and café that sat on the ground floor of one of the grandest office buildings downtown. I marched in and filled out an application and the woman behind the counter looked at me appraisingly and asked a few questions before hiring me on the spot.

The lady who ran the place, a real Little House on the Prairie type woman with blonde hair and blue eyes, took to me and trusted me from the beginning. Having a real job again almost felt like redemption and even though I was just 20 years old, I felt like a kid behind the counter of Casanova Go-Go again, excited to go to work every morning. I was slicing meat, making sandwiches, handling customers and within no time, I started taking on managerial duties.

She had a quirky way of acknowledging and celebrating our work performance and would award us with little pins and ribbons to show others our hard work. With all the pins that I had earned, I looked like a celebrated general. Those pins and my great customer service grabbed the attention of a certain Mr. Jim Marsh, the General Manager of the Summit Club. The Summit Club sat on the top floor of the office building where the Wall Street Deli was located. Until I started working there, I didn't even know that it was a premier fine dining country club, one of those restaurants that would rotate around the top of the building.

What I did know was that Mr. Marsh, a slim and well-groomed man, would come down on a regular basis to get yogurt from the deli and sometimes, we would chat for a little while as he ate it before returning to the top floor. He noticed my pins of recognition that had me looking like a Restaurant General and commented that it looked like I was doing a really good job. One day, he told me that if I ever wanted a real job, I should take the elevator to the top floor and ask to see him.

It took me months of hyping myself up and then bringing myself back down with my own feelings of inadequacy before I finally decided to take him up on his offer. Half a year after I had started working at the Deli, I secured myself a second job working nights at the Summit Club.

It was a place that oozed luxury from every nook and cranny, with rich wood paneling, chandeliers and crystal glasses, and waitresses in formal uniforms. This was no normal restaurant: the restaurant itself spun around the axis of the top floor of the building, providing an unbeatable, rotating view of the city. The guests of the Summit Club were the type of people to travel in private jets and limos and while working there, I met all kinds of people: celebrities, sports stars, politicians.

When I started, the executive chef at the club said that the only thing that I was fit to do there was to wash dishes. His name was Daniel Dovo: he was a world-class chef and his moustache was carefully curled up at the ends. Around his neck, he wore medals of his accomplishments as a French-Canadian chef that made so much noise clanging against each other he sounded like a marching band every time he moved. Chef Dovo was a rigid and stern leader. Before each shift, we would have a line-up meeting where he would check the length of your hair, make sure you had shaved, that your uniform was pressed and cleaned – even us, working back of house in the kitchen, out of sight from the customers.

In my heart. I knew I already had the skills for more than just washing dishes but this was the opportunity I needed to get in the door, and so I accepted the job as a dishwasher. I worked tirelessly at both places, managing the deli from the morning and powering through the menial kitchen tasks the executive chef of the club assigned me at night.

All this time, I was still dealing on the side, nowhere near the same amounts as before back in Michigan, but enough that I was stacking up bread. I paid rent to stay at Auntie Bobbie's, but it was lower than anything else I'd find by myself and so I kept myself busy, working hard enough to ensure that I'd be so tired at night that the floor I slept on felt like a feather mattress. Finally, it paid off and Chef Dovo started giving me more responsibilities and promoting me to line cook so I could start moving my way up the Summit Club's kitchen ranks.

Once he realized that I was more than just a dishwasher, Chef Dovo took a liking to me and took me under his wing. Working in the Summit Club Kitchen, I realized how cocky I had been before, fresh out of school with a vocational diploma and experience from just a handful of small pizzerias and cafeterias. I thought I knew it all but almost every night there were new recipes and foreign ingredients that I had never heard of, let alone seen or tasted before.

Learning how to pronounce the names of new foreign ingredients and techniques was like learning a secret language. I had the most basic skills down but Chef Dovo was quick to let me know when I messed something up. In the beginning, he would cuss me out over sloppy knifework, but I learned fast and in no time, I was chopping vegetables julienne style and breaking down a chicken with a few precise slashes of my knife. He taught me every technique and I memorized every ingredient I touched, knew where the vegetables were grown, and when they were in season; how to butcher different types of meat; where every kind of fish came from, what fat content, salt water, or fresh water.

I picked it up with such ease that the other chefs thought I might have come from an upscale background with experience in fine dining. That was far from being true – my people are as ghetto as they come and I grew up eating soul food: hog, mocks, chitlins, fried fish, fried chicken, mac and cheese, and barbecue ribs. The Summit Club didn't even have a deep fryer.

I didn't know how advanced I became until I left two years later. I started off washing dishes but the time I spent working in that kitchen was like being in real culinary school. My handwriting is still sloppy but I know how to wield a knife better than most people can use a pencil. The skills I learned working there meant that I could survive anywhere in this world.

A little while after I started cooking at the Summit Club, my family held a cookout and I thought to myself, this is my time to flex a little and show them my newly learned skills. I wore an apron over my clothes and standing in front of the smokey barbeque, I asked each of my family members - how would you like your steak cooked? Almost all of them replied to me, "We'll take our steaks well done."

This ain't Chuck E. Cheese, Terrance, don't overcook the steaks, I could hear Chef Dovo hissing in my ear. I used to think beef was supposed to be fully cooked, a little tough and chewy, but at the club, I learned to cook the steaks 'black and blue' and 'Pittsburgh' style, juicy pink in the middle and grilled with gorgeous char marks. I tried to explain to my family that I had learned a better way to cook a steak.

"Cuz, you ain't cooking for them Peckerwood now," my cousin cuffed me in the shoulder and laughed, using

Southern slang we used to talk down to white people. "Burn that damn meat, well done and black!"

Over my shoulder, I could hear Uncle Boot saying to someone else, "All that meat gonna be raw, somebody get that nigga off that grill!"

Auntie Bobbie was always happy to sit and listen to me talk about the club and all the things that I was learning but other people in my family would turn their noses up and change the subject as if to say *we like what we got, we don't want to eat with the white folks.*

Once a year, we would get to invite guests to the club for a meal on the house. I didn't even consider asking any of my family members but Auntie Bobbie overheard me on the phone in her kitchen talking to one of my co-workers about my struggle to find guests to bring to the club and represent me.

Auntie Bobbie said, "I see you calling everyone, trying to get them to go to your job for dinner. Why don't you want me and your uncle to go?" I put my head down, ashamed at myself for not thinking to ask at least her.

From the background in the living room, Uncle Boot shouted, "I ain't going down there with all them peckerwoods."

"You want to come to my job, "Tee Bobbie?" I asked, raising an eyebrow at her and gesturing my head back in Uncle Boot's direction. In my mind, I could see Uncle

Boot cutting up in that country club where I worked so I gave 'Tee Bobbie the tickets. It would be a night to remember for years.

They came to the club dressed to the nines – as long as I'd been staying with them, I hadn't seen them this dressed up. I was standing there to greet them as they exited the elevator and I caught Uncle Boot saying under his breath to my Auntie, "Lord, that's why Alabama ain't got no money. They spending it all here!"

Some of the black servers and bus boys kept coming at me in the kitchen asking, "Them are your people?"

"Yeah!" I'd nod enthusiastically and we'd all laugh and shake our heads in agreement like, *oh boy, this gonna be a good one!*

Once they had been served drinks, their waitress came to me and asked, "Terrence, could you come here for a minute and explain the menu to your family?" I wiggled my eyebrows at everyone in the kitchen as I smoothed out the front of my chef's coat and pushed through the swinging doors to the dining room floor. I described the specials of the night and Uncle Boot ordered the blackened catfish with mango salsa and Auntie Bobbie ordered the chicken fricassee.

I handled their meal in the kitchen with ease and everything was fine until the food hit the table. From where I was standing behind the door, I could see into the dining room but before I could even lay eyes on their table, all I heard was Uncle Boot's voice complaining,

"These hunky's have burned my catfish! And they served it with a fruit salad!"

I dashed to the dining room and asked how they liked their meals. Auntie Bobbie crossed her fork and knife over her plate and said, "I don't like this. It's sour!" Uncle Boot just pointed at his and said, "It's burnt."

I explained to her that her dish was cooked in white wine and capers and to him that the catfish was rubbed in spices and then seared and supposed to look like that. "But if you don't like these, we'll be happy to bring back the menus and make you something else," I finished.

Uncle Boot exclaimed, "Burned up!" and then, "Barbera, get your things! We're going to Captain Dees so I can get me a two-piece fish! This place can't make it no better!"

Chef Dovo surprised me by spending the rest of the night laughing about it. "Terrance," he said to me, "Tell your uncle I'm buying a deep fryer next year just for him."

I continued to stay with my Auntie Bobbie for those four years I lived in Alabama and I was paying rent, putting money in the bank, and eating good by bringing home some of the city's best cuisine. Although I was focused and working harder than I'd ever done before, my uncle – who was generally a good-hearted and hardworking man himself – liked to tease me, calling me a 'Café Ho' in front of his friends and our family.

One night when his friends were over, I came home late from a closing shift and from the living room he called out, "What'd you bring home for us tonight, Café Ho! Snails? Frog legs?"

Maybe my shift had been harder than usual and maybe I was just tired but I'd had enough of listening to that. Without even shrugging my backpack off my shoulders, I came and leaned in the doorway to the living room. "I bet you fifty bucks that if we put our paychecks side by side, I'd be making more than you." It was payday and I knew he wouldn't have had time to cash his yet either.

Uncle Boot had worked in the same US Steel factory for almost his entire adult life, close to thirty years. Well, he put his check down on the table and so did I and there were sighs of disbelief around the room. After all his years of working in the factory I, the one he taunted and called Café Ho, was making more money than him. I never asked him to pay up for losing the bet.

1993-1999: MICHIGAN

For years, I had longed for Alabama and the life I was ripped away from as a child but I found that no matter how hard I tried to fit myself back in that life, it was as though I was a piece that now belonged to a different puzzle. Even though I had reignited my passion for cooking, spent two years working my way up the ranks in the kitchen and for hours at a time managed to forget my past, I realized that I no longer felt like I belonged in Alabama.

To Auntie Bobbie, I claimed noble reasons for quit ting my jobs and packing up and returning to Michigan: I was worried about who was looking out for my siblings because my sister Red, only fifteen years old, had followed in our mother's footsteps and just had a baby. Secretly, I missed the limelight of the hustle: the clubs, the women, the drugs, the money. Some of my buddies back in Michigan who had been in prison were getting out and they had started calling me, telling me that things were popping again, that they had it all set up, that all I needed to do was come home.

I had excellent references from the Summit Club that got me a job at a nice restaurant in Lansing – but when I wasn't at work, I was back in the streets I had grown up in. Not long after I returned to Michigan, one of my boys told me to go down the block to do a deal with somebody he supplied on the regular. He didn't share the details of who I was doing it with.

When I met her, she was standing on a street corner in the projects, pacing back and forth. It was October and the air was crisp and cold. *Damn*, I thought, looking her up and down as I approached her from behind. *She cute.*

Hearing me approaching, she turned around and looked at me directly and asked, "You got something for me?" Her belly was round, a direct mismatch to the rest of her slim frame, and she had to be at least seven months pregnant.

"*Hell* no," I said vehemently, shaking my head and taking a step back. My hands were held up in front of me as though in self-defense. "I ain't dealing with a pregnant lady."

She crossed her arms over her belly and tilted her head to the side, puffing out an irritated sigh. "Look at me - I don't smoke, fool – I'm selling to take care of my baby."

My heart went out to her, this woman selling rocks on the corner to take care of her un-born child and I paused for a beat. I knew what it was like doing whatever it takes to take care of the ones who rely on you – this woman is a survivor. "Yeah," I said, lowering my hands. "I got something."

"How much you got for $200 dollars?"

Slipping my backpack off my shoulder, I thought about how much product was stashed inside and said to her, "I'll give you $600 dollars worth."

"What's the catch?" she asked, narrowing her eyes at me.

I shook my head again and smiled at her. "I'm just looking out for you and your baby."

The next time I met her, a handful of months later, I was passing through a different part of the projects when we made eye contact through an open window. My mind was always on making money, so I immediately thought that where she was staying was a nice hustle spot. Then she said, "Hey," and she smiled at me in recognition and suddenly I could barely remember my own name.

"Hey," I managed to say in return, approaching her window like a prince coming to rescue his princess from the tower.

"I don't think we were properly introduced last time," she said. "My name is Sky – do you wanna come inside?"

Standing in her dimly lit kitchen, I don't know what I expected – but it definitely wasn't that she needed me to watch her baby while she went to social services. It would have been so easy to say *hell no* and get the hell out but her daughter, just a few months old, was already in my arms as her mom pulled on a denim jacket. "Her crib is in the room – thank you – I'll be back soon!" she said and kissed me on the cheek like it was the most normal thing in the world and then right before the door closed behind her she called over her shoulder, "There's beans in the crockpot!"

I held up her daughter to look in her face. "I guess it's just me and you now." She gurgled baby noises back at me in response. I couldn't remember my siblings ever being that small and I rocked her back and forth gently. I took a liking to the baby instantly and I liked the baby mama even more. I put her daughter down for a nap a little later and I managed to put myself to sleep too. When Sky returned home, her beans had burned up. The afternoon sun was now slanting in through the blinds and she found me fast asleep in her bed.

The next thing I knew, I was living there full-time. With her, it didn't matter that her baby daddy was nowhere to be seen, I had already completely accepted my role as father to her daughter. I had raised my siblings since I was just a kid myself and I wasn't afraid of taking care of somebody else's child. Until her, there had been women here and there but never anything that resembled anything close to a serious relationship. Sky was the first time I ever got close enough to choose to live with and love a woman.

We were all over each other like a house on fire. She was the cutest thing I ever saw, sweetest thing I ever tasted and in no time, Sky was pregnant again. Nine months after that, she gave birth to Terry Jr, my son. For a little while, our partnership – our family – was perfect. Before

Jr. was born, she kept selling to her regular customers and I would move behind the scenes, watching her back and keeping her supplied. Afterwards, she stayed home to take care of the babies and I took over the hustle.

After Willie Earl, Shug had some real characters in and out of her life. I would hear about them whenever I spoke to my siblings or aunties. One time she was dating a guy that worked at McDonald's and she ended up breaking up with him for a guy that was a manager at the competition, as though she was moving up in the world, trading in the Golden Arches for the Burger King. I mean everybody got to have someone but I used to ask her, where are you meeting these guys – the damn drive through?

Not long after Terry, Jr. was born, Shug was all set to get married for the third time. It was a big deal because the rest of her family came from Alabama to Michigan to attend. I was nowhere to be found: my contact with her was still minimal around then, I probably hadn't spoken to my mom in years and she had yet to meet her grandson.

Shug was doing her best to pass her new man off to our family, trying to prove that she had found a better man than Willie Earl. He was a nice enough guy on the surface, a former high school track star, but my mom had landed her a full-fledged crack head and we were about to find out just how fast he was.

On the big day, not even a full hour after the ceremony, Shug's new husband slipped out the back door with the bridal purse tucked into the pocket of his all-white tuxedo.

He still hadn't shown his face after a few days and the rest of my family were pissed off and tired of the drama. Auntie Bobbie called me and without even saying hello, said, "You need to get your ass over here."

I thought she was scolding me for not showing up and then I heard Uncle Boot hollering in the background, "Tell Terry to get over here and bring his home boy, that nigga done stole our money!"

"Terrance, I don't care about your reasons for not being here before," Auntie Bird told me. "Get your boys and find that negro. I know you know the areas these type of people be. Go find him and bring back our money." During the entire conversation, I didn't even know what they were talking about but when I got there, I found out that all of my family members had put money envelopes in the bridal purse which Shug's new husband had ran away with.

They knew my reputation, knew that I was a force to be reckoned with on the streets and I was summoned by my family to seek and destroy. I took some ass whoopings but I gave more then I took. My actions were never random acts of malice. Sometimes things happen that have absolutely nothing to do with you and you still gotta deal with it. If you crossed me or my family, I took care of my own.

My boys and I hit the hood hard from north to south, from the east to west side of Lansing. It wasn't hard to find a guy in an all-white Tuxedo. We found him in a crackhouse and he looked like he'd been on a bender since he left the church, tweaking like he hadn't slept for days. His suit wasn't crisp and clean no more and he was so dirty, he looked like he had changed a transmission on a car, more like a mechanic than a groom.

Initially, my first reaction was to beat him down but then I looked at him and I felt pity and sorrow and afraid. I looked at this man and all I saw was me at the same age if I kept going at the same pace as I was. We dragged him outside and two of my boys shoved him in the backseat. He pleaded with us to kill him instead of taking him to face my family but we drove him back to the scene of the crime. Shug was barricaded in her room crying, humiliated because he had made her look like a fool. Their wedding hadn't even been consummated.

I didn't stick around to find out the outcome. My family was mad that he'd already blown through all of the money, disappointed that all I'd done was push him around a little instead of beating him down and hurting him but him and Shug managed to patch things up and stayed married for three years. He was the best one she married, a really nice guy but like Willie Earl, he was on drugs. I saw myself in him and we became friends, hanging out now and then even after him and Shug got divorced, until he died from diabetes.

When Willie Earl got married again, all my brothers and sisters attended his wedding. Willie Earl was the biological father to the twins and Kory, and Red was little enough when he married our mom that he was the only dad she remembered. He was the man who had raised them throughout most of their childhood – even though he was gone half the time and beat them the other half when he was home, they all still call him dad.

His new wife was the same girl that Willie Earl had been cheating on Shug with, and who had ultimately ended their marriage almost a decade ago. Their wedding was held a few months after Shug got remarried and privately I always thought that he only married her to spite Shug, that he just wanted to one-up her one last time.

I stayed by my mom's side and we played cards that day and drank beers together. There weren't many of them, but me and my mom shared some quiet and tender moments together and this one, united in our hatred of Willie Earl, is one of my favorites. She got drunk and on her way to bed, Shug slurred, "The rest of them bitches are traitors but not you, Terry."

I discovered that Shug, even though I had long been an adult, was still collecting back child support payments from

Jimmy Lee Prince. Until I was a young teenager, because of Shug's lies, I had believed that Jimmy Lee Prince was my father and that his mother, who I affectionately called Tha-Boo, was my grandmother. He had even gone to jail for not keeping up with paying child support payments. I had known the truth for years and I confronted Shug about the cruelty of what she was doing to Jimmy, but it only turned into an argument.

She treated my relationship with Tha-Boo and Jimmy like it was nothing. I had returned to Alabama three years earlier and asked her about Tha-Boo's whereabouts so that I could visit her and she coldly said, "That woman is dead." Shug had used them like pawns and disregarded them like pawns. She told me that on Jimmy Lee's deathbed, he had tried to call her and she had not picked up the phone. Seven days later, they found Jimmy Lee in his home, dead and decomposed.

The shame that I had held for my mother's lies regarding my biological father had kept me away from my beloved Tha-Boo and Jimmy Lee for most of the rest of their lives. I avoided them as much as I could because I could not bear to look them in their faces knowing she had manipulated them. I knew that I was not responsible for her actions but the shame that I associated with her actions made me want to escape my reality, made me want to get high.

I'm pretty sure that people in the neighborhood back in Alabama who knew of Sam and my Mom's relations speculated that perhaps Jimmy wasn't my dad. Looking back on my life and knowing what I know now, I still feel that way and I still consider Jimmy my father and Tha-Boo my grandmother because they claimed me as theirs and never defaulted on me or denied me, even though the truth was probably blowing through the wind of Loveman Village, the projects where Tha-Boo cared for me, helped raise me, and carried me around.

When Sky and I were good, God, we were so good, could barely keep our hands off each other. But when we were bad – we truly brought out the worst in each other. The thing about a burning house is that unless somebody puts it out, it will burn itself to the ground. Sky got bored of being a stay-at-home mom quick and I found out that she had a possessive streak. She knew that I was in the streets hustling, a job that has no office hours, but if I wasn't home when she wanted me to be, she'd start arguments when I did show up, shouting at me until we took it to the bedroom to make up.

One time, Sky pushed the sofa up against the door so that I couldn't come in without dealing with her. She set up camp and slept there on the sofa, anticipating my arrival, ready for a fight. But her strategy had a flaw. Because she was a hard sleeper and when I came home that night, I just shoved the door, the couch, and her to the side, letting myself in without waking her up. Pushing the couch back into position in front of the door, I admired her for a moment and then kissed her still sound asleep forehead, then went into the bedroom and fell asleep on the bed.

As a light sleeper myself, in the wee hours of the morning when the sun was barely up, I startled awake to hear her already on the phone with her friend, telling them, "He ain't even home yet! Hoo boy, he don't even know what's coming for him!"

I listened for a little while, letting her wind herself up and get good and mad and then, I came strolling out of the bedroom holding the babies.

Sky stared at me for a moment, speechless, and said into the phone, "I gotta go." And then to me, "How the fuck did you get in here?" she demanded, outraged I had outsmarted her and I just gave her a silly smirk and passed her a baby as I kissed her cheek, ready to argue until she tired herself out and wanted something else.

Before we met and before she started dealing, Sky had been a professional fighter and she was always prepared for a violent confrontation. When other girls came swinging like a windmill, she'd be throwing combinations, uppercuts, and body shots. She was the Rio Road Tasmanian Devil – she would go after anybody and was known for beating up niggas and bitches alike with a record of wins against 30 bitches and 5 niggas.

Sky was 135 pounds of aggression: she liked to fight, maybe even more than she liked to fuck. Her rage was fueled by jealousy and combined with her pro fists and a short temper – she was lethal. Growing up, she had been abused and forced to learn how to protect herself and she repeated the patterns of violent outbursts and make-ups. I was deeply unhappy to have somehow landed myself back into a violent and manipulative household. When I got tired of her temper lashing out and even more tired of arguing back, I started sleeping around and using drugs heavily again. Sky's reputation preceded me and even though we were on again, off again, regularly by the end, it was next to impossible to get a woman to even entertain the idea of sleeping with me if they knew that she was my girlfriend.

When she'd hear about me sleeping around, cheating on her, physical fighting wasn't enough for her either. I don't even remember how many times she called the police on me during a fight, giving them a story of me attacking her so that they would haul me off to jail, even though I had defensive wounds all over my body from fending her off. Then she'd jump in the car and be trailing the police all the way to the police station to bail me out, arguing with and cussing at the police when they questioned her about what happened, just so we could pick up the fight where we left it off when we got back in the car.

During our relationship, I had never been sexed and sucker punched so much in my life. Eventually, we couldn't have enough make-up sex to fix all the fighting. Three years after we met, we broke up for good and I packed my things in a backpack and I left her and my son behind.

I had been smoking crack here and there throughout our relationship, always in what I had considered a very controlled, moderate way. For the entire decade I had been dealing and smoking crack, I was able to convince myself that I wasn't a true addict because I never owned my own pipe. People I hung out with knew that I'd share whatever I had on me if they'd let me use their pipe. When I felt like I was in control, just a hit would be enough, and I'd still be able to walk away and go home and keep up appearances. I almost always had a job in a restaurant while I sold drugs on the side, which meant that I ate good with staff meals during shifts and kept myself looking healthy.

But after I left Sky, she started using the kids as pawns and keeping them from me, which sent me deeper into my addiction. I started seeing signs that I was only the shadow of the person I used to be. It became harder and harder to walk away from the drugs and I started crashing on dingy mattresses in crack houses, just so that there would always be someone around with a pipe. I had given up on how I looked and dressed and even though I was still working in a kitchen at the time, I had stopped eating regularly so my weight had diminished. One time I was dehydrated so bad I passed out in front of my sister's place and she called the ambulance and I spent three days in the hospital.

On multiple occasions if they didn't hear from me, my sisters would hunt me down, knocking on the doors of my last known location and interrogating my friends to find out where I was at so they could drag my ass away from crack houses and drug attics.

My sister came to pick me up from my job one day and I saw that she had borrowed Willie Earl's car. Twisting around to toss my backpack into the backseat, I noticed a pair of shoes tucked underneath the driver's seat. My own sneakers were beat down and I badly needed a new pair; I reasoned that he had gotten me addicted to crack and a fair exchange ain't no robbery. When she went into the house, I told her I forgot something and went back to the car and grabbed them.

Willie Earl called Shug when he found out I had taken his shoes, accusing me of thievery to fuel my addiction. They had both remarried and were living their own lives; I only could imagine how the conversation started about me. I hadn't seen them in the same room together in years and walking into the old house and seeing them on the couch together sent me straight back to my childhood to arguments that escalated into beatings – except that now, I was an adult, and my mom and ex-stepfather called me there for an intervention.

"Terry, sit down," Shug started first. "Terry, I'm so disappointed in you – I had no idea – it hurts me to see you like this," she said in a heavy voice, "Terry, you are my oldest child and your brothers and sisters are afraid you're going to die."

Part of me wondered if she was crying crocodile tears, but my heart ached at her words.

Then Willie Earl announced, "Me and your mom didn't raise you like this. Who are these people that you've been running with?" he demanded as though he hadn't hit me up to hook him up, as though he hadn't personally handed the pipe to me. "Who you selling for?"

If he thought for one second I was going to let him ride past me on a high horse, he was dead wrong. I really don't know if he even knew what the truth was anymore. I had kept his secret for way too long. All these years, I let all the blame and humiliation fall on me and people always wondered who introduced me to crack cocaine or assumed it was because I was selling. Willie Earl forced me to break my silence and let all the shit fly.

"Shut the *fuck* up," I snarled. I wasn't the little boy you could put in a full nelson and make me submit to your will, I was a fully grown man, in that moment, ready to fight a war. I said, "Mama, you know this mother fucker right here give me crack when I was seventeen," and then, my voice suddenly soft and young sounding, "I had never even smoked weed or a cigarette a day in my life and then my first drug was crack cocaine."

Shug barely reacted, just asked with a blank look on her face, "Why did you try it?"

I didn't know how to explain it to her. Even though I was selling and had seen the havoc it wreaked on people's lives in their desperate need to get more, somehow when he offered it to me, I never thought of it as him giving me the most powerful drug in the world at that time. I thought it was Willie Earl finally wanting to spend time with me, like it was some kind of fucked up inevitable ceremony to welcome me to the only type of manhood that I had witnessed growing up.

Instead, I said to her sharply, "You knew he was using." Her eyes got big and she opened her mouth to deny it but I continued over her, accusing, "It's your fault. I heard Granddaddy beg you not to go to Michigan with him. I heard him say that this man had just left his family with four young boys in New York. And you took us to another state with him, what the hell were you thinking? You should've packed us up and took us back to Alabama when you saw what he brought us to. Look at us, around a bunch of people we don't know and with no family."

It seemed like both she and Willie Earl were lost for words, mouths gaping open like fish out of water. I said, "You know why he did this to me, mom? Because I was your bread and butter. You see? I kept you afloat for years but he wanted you to fail. I was your shining star, so how do you shoot down a shining star?" With tears in my eyes, I said, "You don't give someone you love a drug like this."

Finally, speechless myself, I told them to get up. We went out front and I took his shoes right off my feet and I threw them at his car. I walked down the street on the sidewalk, small stones on the pavement cutting into my bare feet. I didn't turn back to see if they watched me go and me, Willie Earl, and Shug never spoke about it again.

Although I had been dismissive of my mom and Willie Earl's intervention, deep down I knew that I couldn't go on like this. I tried to get help for my addiction, I called all the treatment facilities in the area, but each time got the same response: that I didn't have insurance and I couldn't get funding for my treatment. I made several attempts to get into rehab but it was next to impossible without insurance.

One kind receptionist that I spoke to on the phone said if a family member had insurance, I could be eligible to receive treatment. My mom was a schoolteacher so I knew she had insurance and I felt a spark of hope. But when I brought it to her attention, I found out that she had been using her insurance to put her third husband through treatment and that her insurance wouldn't cover anymore treatment. "How many times have you paid for his treatment?" and her only response was "You shouldn't have tried crack anyway."

Drugs like heroin, which were used primarily by white kids, had funding for rehabilitation and treatment. But crack, a drug predominantly used in black communities, didn't have the same type of recovery options. My only option was to depend on the system for help and the only form that help came in was prison, by committing a crime under the court's jurisdiction. I was busy in the streets at the time, so I knew I had a warrant for my arrest for something or another.

It was common in those days to give a guy a rock in exchange for the use of their car and drive it until the wheels fell off, but this time, I had rented a car from a guy whose wife worked for the City of Lansing and overextended my use of it. She had called the police and reported her car stolen. It was three of us in the car, making sales and seeing what other hustles we could do. The police spotted us, pulled us over, and we were all charged with joy riding. I was able to turn myself in on these charges in hopes of getting help with my addiction.

For over a month I was in the county jail waiting for my court date. I was having dreams about getting high. Right before I pulled on the pipe and felt sweet relief, I would wake up, sweating and heart racing, to the guard yelling over the PA system, "Cell checks, off the phone, out the shower, prepare for count!" I was struggling with craving crack but I was relieved to not have a heroin addiction. I watched other men in the jail going through heroin withdrawal and that drug was more physical than mental. They would be sick for days while going through detox, shaking, throwing up, losing control over bowel movements.

A kid I knew from the neighborhood had a visitor and when he came back to our cell block, he told me that he saw my mom waiting in the visiting room. I shrugged at him outwardly, but inside I was ecstatic that my mom was coming to the jail to check on me – maybe she had actually meant the things she said when she staged the intervention.

I waited and waited for them to call my name. After an hour, I began to think the guards were blocking her from coming to see me, so I disrupted their cell check and refused to go back in my cell until my mom was allowed to visit me. What could they do to me? I was already in jail, I didn't have any money and I was at the mercy of the system. They couldn't take my phone privileges, commissary, or visitation because nobody accepted my phone calls, nobody sent me money, and nobody came to see me. A little while later, the guard announced over the PA system, "Wallace, your mother didn't come to see you, she came to see someone on Post 7." I shouldn't have been surprised, but I was: she had not come to see me, she was visiting her third husband and didn't leave me a dime in my commissary. I was ashamed of myself for getting my hopes up and hurt and realized that I had to get better for me, because all I had was myself.

My court appointed attorney came to see me and I was completely honest with him. I explained my history and addiction to crack and asked him could he have the judge put me in treatment. I didn't even know what treatment was, I didn't know if they would give me a pill to make me better, but I was game for anything at this point. I began to ask questions about going to a rehabilitation program.

I was recognizing more and more that I had a serious drug problem. I had a good skill set, I was very employable and I was charismatic, funny, and very easy to get along with, but I just couldn't manage my life. Several guys who had accepted that they had an addiction told me about good programs that had much success; they sat and talked with me about where they had gone wrong in their recovery and were very eager to try it again. I didn't understand any of this at the time but recovery is not a one-shot deal. It's a process, like a toddler learning to walk: you don't start running, you scoot, you crawl, you hold on to stuff, you stumble, you fall down, and when you fall, you get back up and you try it again.

I went before the judge and for the first time in my life, I did not deny any of my involvement. I explained to the judge presiding over the hearing that I turned myself in because I needed help. He asked me if I had a program in mind. I had the name written on a jail kite (internal memo) so I wouldn't forget it. The program was called Alternative Directions, in Grand Rapids, a city known as the city for second chances. The punishment for my crime was 180 days in jail or a $5000 fine and I had to pay the car owner for missing work because we were joy riding in her car and it was ordered by the court that I would do 180 days at this program. As I looked around, I could see everyone in the court room silently wishing me well. As to not disrupt the court, they gave me kind gestures of affirmation, thumbs up, head nods, and looks of encouragement. Even the judge wished me well as I left the stand.

I was driven 68 miles away from Lansing and dropped off in Grand Rapids where I would spend six months participating in the Alternative Directions rehabilitation program. Even though it was just an hour away, I had never been there before and I had no idea what Grand Rapids had in store for me, but I did know that I had to look forward and not look back. It was a matter of life and death.

Once I got settled into the program, it wasn't the setting that I had hoped for. It wasn't a very supportive atmosphere. Within the group, I could not express myself or ask questions about recovery among my peers. Most of the guys were there against their will, I was the only one in that program that had any type of willingness to be there. I only felt comfortable expressing my deepest feelings in one-on-one counselling; however, you can't get the real answers that you are looking for from someone who has never experienced the grip of addiction.

During my first one-on-one session, the counsellor asked me a series of questions. She asked about my family and how I was raised and as I answered, I broke down like a baby and I cried for an hour and she even cried with me. The emotional release felt like a relief, but crying did me no good. I had to get out there, I had to get back to where I was before crack had taken over my life and flush all the street behaviors out of my system.

I told the counsellor about my passion and previous experience in the culinary world. She assigned me to work in the kitchen and the food that I made was phenomenal.

I was an instant hit and even the staff started to stay to eat instead of going out for meals. Good food makes people smile and some of the female staff started harmlessly flirting with me, giving me a much-needed confidence boost. They encouraged me, suggesting places I should apply, saying, "Your food is amazing, you're not going to have any problem getting a job!"

For the first time in three years, I was crack free. I had 90 days under my belt, my weight came back and I was looking like myself again. This was the first attempt to have a life without drugs or even attempt to hustle. As long as I was not trying to sell drugs, I could keep my addiction under control and function as a normal person would, but once I saw the drugs, my heart would start racing and my palms would start to sweat. I was still very new in my recovery and still learning my triggers. I put together my resume and was given bus passes to look for work and pointed in the direction of downtown Grand Rapids.

I got myself a job interview at the most beautiful hotel in Grand Rapids, the Amway Grand Plaza. I learned that the sous chef was from Lansing during the interview and I thought, with him and I being from a common area I would have an advantage, but that was not the case. He drilled me on questions and terminology. I was asked a series of cooking questions, what was my style of cooking, and from what regions of the world were my favorite recipes.

I knew how to make mostly anything but I was not versed in the terminology of cooking, which is what distinguishes a chef from a cook. I couldn't state not one recipe. I named some dishes that sounded good but when he asked me what ingredients went into them, I blanked. I could not answer one question without the assistance of the executive chef who was trying to help me out, but the sous chef insisted that he let me answer on my own.

Afterwards, to defend myself I blurted out, "I know I bombed the interview but if you let me in the kitchen, I will *show you* what I have underneath the hood."

The executive chef asked, "When can we take you up on that offer?" and I responded confidently, "Right now."

As I walked on the line, I felt confident and I felt at home. I hadn't been in a commercial kitchen in what felt like forever and I had read their menu and it was a piece of cake. In my interview, I requested the sauté station, the most skilled position in the kitchen. The kitchen positions are grill chef, who is responsible for cooking steaks, chicken, fish and other grilled items. Then you have the pantry chef who is in charge of desserts, salads, and some appetizers. The chef at the fry station cooks all deep-fried items, then you have the sauté chef who is responsible for soups, sauces, and all sautéed items, this position brings all the flavors together in the kitchen and then you have the expediter who is the director of the show, who makes sure all the food goes out in a timely manner and is directed to each table.

The sous chef stood in the corner and glanced over at me. As the tickets began to roll off the printer, he began to call off the items. I was cooking with the speed of a cheetah. They couldn't call off the orders fast enough. I knew what items went with each meal, I knew which items were hot items, which items were just there to fill the menu, and based on my experience and my intuition, I even knew if the guest ordering was a male or female, or even the nationality or ethnicity of the guest. If you saw three well done steaks on the ticket, it was some brothers in the house and burn it till it's black or they gon' send it back.

I was working the whole line and even stepped up to the expediter position, but I wasn't rude or trying to overthrow his position, I just needed to flex the power that I possessed and show what I was capable of. I began to call off the appetizers to the other chefs so they could start the ticket. At the beginning of the meal, we send out the bread to pacify you and curb the appetite, and then your salad, then you get your sorbet to cleanse your palate, then comes the main course, and finally the dessert. You do not want your appetizers to come up with the rest of your food. Each course should be timed to show that the kitchen is cooking in a timely manner.

After the rush, all eyes were bucked and all mouths were wide open. I thanked everyone for letting me work with them and a few guys asked if I was the new chef. As

I raised my head to respond to them, I caught the sous chef's eye and replied, "I hope so."

I was led back to the executive chef's office again where the interview had taken place and both him and the sous chef started to look over my application again with a fine-tooth comb. The sous chef asked where I got my training and who trained me. I described my time in Alabama working at the Summit Club under Chef Daniel Dovo and the sous chef stated, "Well, he did you an injustice." I was shocked, expecting praise and that took the spark away from me for a moment. "Dovo was a lazy chef, he taught you a skill set, he made you a work horse, but he did not teach you the terminology. You have raw talent, the best I've seen in a long time." He continued, "Now, Mr. Wallace, I'm willing to teach you terminology to add to your skill set. Are you up for challenge? The first thing I want you to do is go see Angus Campbell at the community college and enroll yourself in culinary school. We have a scholarship program and this hotel will sponsor you. You have raw talent."

Grand Rapids is a culinary town, it had the best junior college culinary program in the United States. I had gone in hoping for a job at best but I walked out with not only a job, but a ride to an esteemed culinary program. The talent in that town is unimaginable and that same talent had been recognized in me.

There was only one person back home in Lansing who truly cared about my well-being: my little sister, Red. She would call me and I would tell her about my progress, and when I was nearing the end of the program, she told me that she would come pick me up and take me home. I said to her, "Red, I'm not coming back there. I'm staying here in Grand Rapids."

I was 45 days from being released on my own and I had completed all the requirements of the program. My time in the program was coming to an end. I had gotten myself a job that I loved, I was attending the community college, and NA and AA meetings. But the prospect of being in the real world outside of the program scared me because I was still having crack dreams where I would wake up just before I pulled on the pipe. Even the sight of someone smoking a cigarette was enough to make my heart skip a beat. Most people in program were in a rigid setting so it was easy to follow the program, either you followed the program, or you went back to jail – and back to jail wasn't an option for me. As long as I was working and staying busy, I could control my urges.

"Where are you going to live?" she asked. "What will you do! You don't know nobody there."

"I'll figure it out," I told her and I asked a few guys at work for some advice on where I could get hired as a night chef. Their reply was just to throw your resume in the air and by the time it hits the ground, you'll have a job.

I got myself a second job at the B.O.B., the Big Old Building. It was not only big but also bold, standing 4 stories tall, with 70,000 square feet and made of red bricks. When you want something to last, you build it of brick. When I asked questions about it, I was told it used to be a grocery warehouse and had been vacant for decades, about to be torn down until a man named Greg Gilmore saw its potential and revived it, creating the best restaurants in the city out of nothing. The B.O.B. as I knew it was a space with a lot of variety and a lot of hustle and bustle. It had all the elements of the phrase eat, drink, and be merry all under one roof: there were numerous restaurants and venues for dining, comedy, and live music – Gill's Fish House, Judson's Steakhouse, the Pig Pit, the Monkey Bar, Eve's Club, Dr. Grin's Comedy Club, and a microbrewery. I had never been part of an operation like this with so much talent in the building and I was happy to be there among such great chefs.

I was placed in Gills Fish House in a skilled position in a two-man kitchen. I learned and studied the menu until I knew it inside and out; this was the kind of kitchen where they called for the food and plate and you had to remember and then call back the item. I worked side by side with Slayer. He started the food order, seasoned it, and sautéed the fish items and my job was to finish and plate. Slayer was the actual Gordon Ramsey before there was a Gordon Ramsey. He was hard on servers and if they messed up an order, they were sent running in tears. He was so talented that his behavior was overlooked, but then there was me and I refused to take his shit – it was only a matter of time before we bumped heads.

When I had worked there for a while, I heard that there was a position opening up at Judson's Steak House. Judson's was the crème de la crème of the B.O.B. Judson's had a prize kitchen and working there included a substantial raise. The executive chef over the whole operation at the B.O.B was Chef Todd Darby, a big Indian man who had never been to culinary school. He had come into the company from the ground up and there was loyalty in him. I knew I had to be on point to show Todd my worth. One Friday, our busiest day, we knew that we would be extra busy because Floyd Mayweather was hosting an All-Star Basketball Game at the Van Andel Arena which was built for live entertainment and sporting events. There were celebrities from all over the country, Cedric the Entertainer, 50 Cent, Jadakiss, Lloyd, Lil Fizz, B2K, Kid Capri, Spinderella, Swiss Beatz, Keyshia Cole, Soulja Boy, and Chili of TLC.

I came in an hour early just to prep. I wouldn't have to leave the line to grab nothing. The tickets from the machine started to flow and it was printing so fast, we thought it was broken. Slayer raged, accusing the servers of not putting their tickets in on time and slamming the machine with orders, but that wasn't the case. We were just that busy and there would be no excuses, it was ass and elbows that night. Slayer intimidated the other expeditors and usually Todd never worked the window, but tonight, Chef Todd was there to intervene.

Todd began to bark off the orders. He called for it, I repeated the order and gave a time frame. "One minute chef, 2 minutes chef, on item #2. Chef, item #3 is not fired. Items 3-13 have not been fired, Chef." Todd shouted through the window back at me, "Fire the items then!" I entered Slayer's territory as respectfully as I could and then I began to step in his space, and he could feel my presence. He really couldn't say anything because Todd was watching and the window was completely full of tickets. The B.O.B. had a guarantee that all food would be served within 15 minutes and tonight we were determined to honor that.

At one point, Todd caught my eye and gave me a nod, urging me to push harder and I began to apply pressure. He had established a line of communication with me and in that moment, it was me and him. I started calling for food items and Slayer's only reply was, "Working."

"Chef, I'm missing this item. Food is dying here!" Todd kept calling at me through the window.

Again, I asked Slayer, "How long?"

"When I fucking give it to you," Slayer said without looking up.

I stopped everything and I said, "What the fuck did you just say to me?" Suddenly we were faced off, practically standing nose to nose.

"Y'all done crying yet?" Todd yelled. "Give me the fucking food!"

We worked the rush until it died down. Throughout the rest of the night there were glimpses and side looks, and under the breath conversations about the face off that had happened between me and Slayer. All the servers came to me and said good job. Nobody had stood up to him and showed him up. That night I was seen. Everybody including Slayer *actually* saw me – most importantly, Chef Todd.

After the rush, Todd told me he wanted me to come to his office. For a brief moment, I was like, *oh shit, I'm fired*, but no. He explained to me that I had really shown what I could do and I was offered the sous chef job at Judson's. I told Todd about my past and that I would soon be leaving the rehab program. He was beyond supportive and said that kitchens were no strangers to drugs and alcoholics, a place for misfits to fit right in, where we all come together as one family.

I made a home for myself in Grand Rapids. Another chef that I worked with help me find housing. I had a new relationship, my first girlfriend since Sky. I was responsible for the first time in a long time, I enrolled in school and I struggled severely but I didn't quit. I was working two jobs and attending school. It was one of the greatest times of my life; it was a time of restoration and I was doing well. I had great coworkers and as much work as I wanted between the Grand Plaza and the B.O.B. I had money and a glimmer of hope that I would survive crack, but my past wouldn't stay at bay for long.

My sisters began to come to Grand Rapids, showing up uninvited whenever they pleased. Our mom had admitted defeat and abandoned ship, moving back to Alabama. For the first time, they were without their foundation and life was showing my sisters a hard time; Red had two young boys of her own with no skill set and welfare was her only means of support. There was pressure for me to return to Lansing to reassume my role as the big brother and family head.

Chef Todd was pissed when he found out that I resigned from my jobs and quit school. He said, "You've come so far, why would you go back there?" My only answer was that my family needed me. The words he said to me as I left still echo around my brain: "You can't build a house on quicksand."

I had been gone from Lansing for two years. Shug had given up and returned to Alabama; she left her house up for grabs to anyone and me and Uncle Bill lived there until the mortgage company foreclosed on the house. I was clean and I had gained weight again. I got a head chef job at a restaurant called Pistachios where I ran a crew of eight people, a good set of guys working for me. But I didn't give my skill the credit it deserved.

People in the hood started seeing me around and they asked me, "You got back on?" and I was like, "Yeah man, I got my shit back tight." I knew a lot of drug dealers from back in the day and I was still connected. I tricked myself back onto the streets and I started using again and missing shifts at work. I was moving drugs for most of the people on the north side of Lansing. I still had a ghetto pass and I was welcomed in every hood.

What the other men in the program had told me about relapsing made sense to me in a whole new way. I was in complete misery and I had let myself down. The only difference in me from before I went to rehab in 1997 to 1999 is that I now had fresh clothes and I was just a dressed-up crackhead. I didn't dream about drugs anymore, I dreamed about my peace and my new life that I had built just to leave behind.

I backslid so hard that I crash landed into rock bottom. Out of all the years of me getting high, I never owned a pipe. I insisted that having a pipe made me a full-blown crack head and I convinced myself that it wasn't like that for me. After doing drugs on and off for so many years, I had gotten tired of sharing my drugs, telling people "I'll give you some to use your pipe." After all the hustle and what I did all day to obtain my drugs, I would always have to share it with someone else because I refused to have my own. As my addiction spiraled, what little pride I had left disappeared and I bought my first pipe at the store on the corner. I accepted that I crossed the line and truly was an addict. They called it a set up: for five bucks, you get the full package - the screen, lighter, and pipe. I thought maybe if I had my own pipe, I'll have enough drugs.

As luck would have it, on the first day of me owning this pipe, it slipped out of my pocket, undetected by me. Uncle Billy found the pipe tucked in between the couch cushions and in retaliation, he locked me out of my mom's house.

When I returned home after double shifts to find the door locked, I heard people inside and I banged desperately on the door. My uncle shouted from the top window, "Get away from here, crackhead!" It hurt me to my soul for my uncle to call me that. "Take your crackhead ass down the street."

Tears streamed down my face that I had no power to stop. I yelled back, "If Grandaddy and Ma Dear had taken care of me I wouldn't be like this." I paused, my voice wavering, "I need help, Bill, please help me. I don't know what to do. I feel like dying. I don't want to be like this."

I stayed in an abandoned house that night and I was so cold and angry that at around 6am, I couldn't take it no more. I picked up bricks as I walked towards my mom's house and then I went around to every window in that house and I started throwing bricks in each window. I screamed until my voice was hoarse, "Bill – mother fucker, if I'm going to be cold you bitches are going to be cold too." The house was being foreclosed on and if he wouldn't let me in, I was just going to expedite his moving out process. After that, I stayed at the homeless shelter.

Crack was like a bad girlfriend, constantly calling on me at all hours and wanting all my time and money. The only thing that could quiet her summoning and bring my mind peace was working. I worked two jobs, sometimes as much 16 hours a day, ducking and dodging her calls, filling my days to avoid the urge to use. I would hate days off from work with nothing to distract myself and paydays were even worse because with money in my pocket, the temptation to buy it was that much stronger. Sometimes I was stronger than my urges and I could last it out, but more times I let myself slide, let myself get seduced by crack, arguing that this time, this is the last time I go back to her.

Down to my bones, I was tired of it. My eyes were so blood shot I must have permanently looked like a deer in the headlights. I wanted it all to stop. How could I fix this?

I had gone into the bank to cash my check from work and I stood there feeling the dread of getting paid and having a day off. When I approached the bank teller's window, I recognized her as someone who I went to school with. She greeted me warmly but she was called away and motioned for me to wait as she stepped away from the window, leaving an entire stack of cash just within my grasp.

I knew it was wrong, but the drugs were an incessant whispering at the back of my head even on a good day, and now it was like a beautiful woman snaking her arms around my waist, talking right in my ear, demanding and seductive. *They can't see you. Steal the money.* I tried to tell myself that I knew it was wrong. Crack reassured me, *they can't see you, they'll never know.* Her claws dug in me so deep and the idea filled my brain like smoke. *Think how good it'll feel.* I reached into the small opening of the teller's window as her back was turned and I grabbed half of the stack of bills and stuffed it in my pocket.

A friend of mine had gone to prison and come out a different man. I thought that if nobody could help me, maybe prison was my way out. It wasn't premeditated or planned, I happened to be in the right place at the right time and opportunity made me a thief. Stealing the money was a calculated sacrifice – I wanted to get caught, wanted to be sent to prison.

Even though I was weary, tired to the bone, when I wasn't working, I was bursting with uneasy restless energy and this made it that much worse. I could have sworn the money was literally burning a hole in my pocket, making me fidget as my eyes darted around the room. The teller returned to the window and none the wiser of my actions, helped me cash my check and then pleasantly said thank you and have a good day.

I was on TV, on the news on a daily basis. The news was saying that I robbed the bank and I was on Michigan's most wanted, and it felt like the entire state was looking for me. I stayed on the run for two weeks, moving in the shadows from neighborhood to neighborhood, staying at motels and crashing with friends. Then my 'friends' turned me in once I ran out of money.

When the police handcuffed me and placed me in the back of the police raid van, I was happy, almost laughing, floating – high on her. As I leaned my head back and tried to look through the roof of the car to the sky, I said to nobody, "Hi crack, I'm going to beat you, we're done. I don't care how long they keep me, but this part of my life is over."

Once I was booked and had a few hours to sleep, when I woke up, I expected to hear her, Crack, continuing to talk to me and comfort me in her own sick twisted way, but I no longer heard her voice. I was already craving and calling her, but she was nowhere to be found. I called her name and she did not respond. When I came down off that high, I was scared and shaking and relieved because I realized that this was my time to regain my sobriety.

The arresting officer knew me: he was the same cop who had slammed me on the ground outside the Adidas warehouse all those years ago. He had made sergeant and he and his partner came to the cell afterwards to talk to me. He told his partner to leave the room so he could talk to me by myself.

Finally, I cried and let it all out. He explained to me I could get help while I was serving my prison sentence. I wasn't exactly happy about going to prison, I wanted to take off running, knowing that I had just broken the law and was probably facing some serious time. But I was happy to be alive and getting help. When I was in prison,

I got a hundred bucks put in my account from someone. I know in my heart it was Officer Garcia.

I took my case to trial because they were trying to give me 20 years for robbing the bank and having intimidating posture, when I never intimidated anyone, either verbally or nonverbally. I reached behind the counter and took the money. I didn't rob the bank, I just stole. I had to convince them that what they were attempting to charge me with, did not coincide with what I did. I was guilty and I needed to be put away to get help, but I didn't want to go away forever.

The judge gave me 56 to 120 months. I didn't even know how much time it was, I had to count it out on my fingers. As I calculated on my fingers, I said to the judge, "Your honor, I can't do all that time!" The judge said, "Do the best you can, son, and the rest will come easy." That's how they thought about sending you to prison. They didn't care less.

2014 Atlanta, GA
Edna Lewis Foundation
Gala at the Le Cordon
Bleu Culinary College

2015 Atlanta, GA with Mike Epps

2015 Miami, FL with Ivan Zoot,
fastest barber in the world

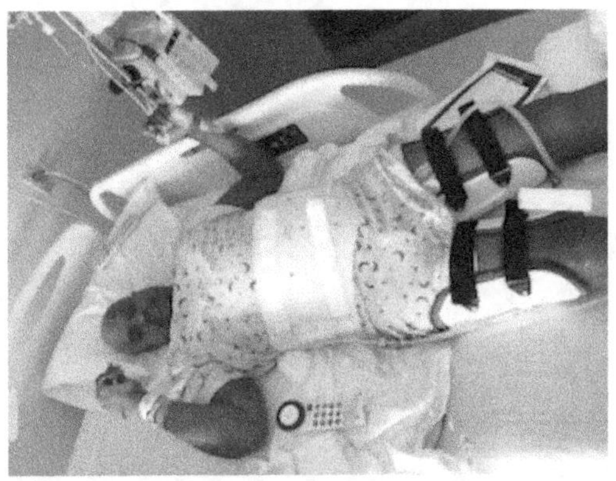

2017 on the radio in the
US Virgin Islands

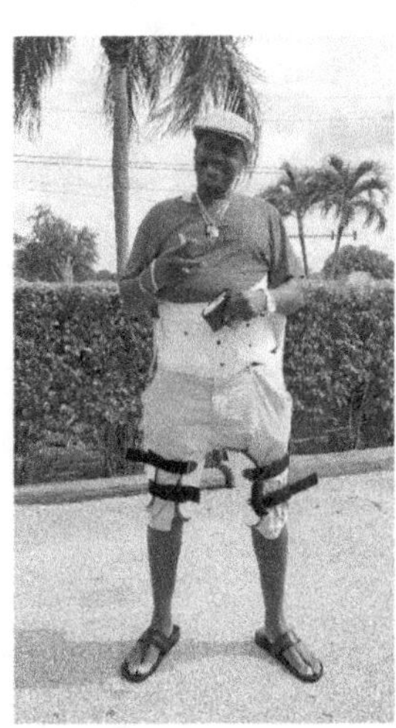

2017 West Palm Beach, FL
Second spinal surgery

During Prison

2001-2008: MICHIGAN

Imagine eight city blocks, six stories high, filled with nothing but bird cages. It was like coming out of the tunnel into a football stadium, but instead of adoring fans there were angry prisoners screaming and yelling from every direction. The noise was overpowering, people trying to get your attention for you to come to their cell. My cell was on the third floor. There was no privacy, six rows of cells stacked sky high – you could see clear across from one side to the other, guys pacing back and forth, working out, sitting on the toilet, literally everything.

They didn't call you by your name, they called you by a number, a series of digits you never forget. My number was 374084. After 20 years, I remember that number just like my social security number. In my cell that first night, it felt like this was it, the next eight years of my life and I doubted I could survive this. Over the next days, other guys explained to me that this is just a quarantine period where you wait while they figure out what prison to place you in long term. I'd be sent somewhere else – this is where murderers spend their time, my custody level wasn't high enough to be here. But before they told me, I was trying to come up with ways to end my life.

During quarantine everybody has to get a medical exam: see a psychologist, get a physical, get your shots, eye

136

tests, blood work. They ask you about educational history and what you did before prison. Most guys were like, well, that's why I'm here. But I had a lot on my resume, I went to vocational school, got a GED, I cook.

The prison counsellor asked me, "Well, what are you doing here?"

Even just admitting the truth out loud is one of the hardest parts. I took a deep breath and I said, "I'm addicted to crack." And then I started crying.

"You can come out here a better person or a worse person, it's up to you," she said. "Prison doesn't have to be a punishment." She showed me some pamphlets about the various programs the prisons offered that could help me get myself together. Cooking courses, computer classes, AA, NA, self-help groups. It gave me new hope. It gave me will to live. She told me when I got to my prison, to tell them what I can do and she was sure I'd be able to get a job in the prison.

During the quarantine period, for around two months, they shuffled me around the state between different prisons, before I landed at a place near home where I'd serve almost all my time. The uniform at this prison was navy blue with an orange stripe down the side. The rooms were like a military barrack, rows of bunk beds all over the room. Each dorm housed 200 inmates at a time with eight dorms in the prison. The guys who been in there a long time got the bottom bunks, forcing the newbies to the top. Lights out were at 10pm. Outside, the grass was cut nice and there were flower beds between some of the dorms. If it weren't for the fences and guards keeping us imprisoned, it almost felt like what I imagined summer camp to be like as a child.

After all the medical and psychological tests they make you go through during quarantine, the long term prison still makes you go through skills and abilities tests to get a prison plan before they can offer any job placements, a process that takes approximately 6 months. Making time pass every single day was a battle.

The prison was filled with faces I knew from the streets, kids I used to know who'd turned into men behind bars. I did my best to stay out of their way, wouldn't hang with the old crew on the inside because they were stuck in old habits, still selling and doing drugs, drinking, gambling, stealing. The only thing that you don't have access to in prison is women on a daily basis – and even then, certain female guards were known for more…sexperimental rehabilitation therapy. I wasn't entertaining the hood, glamorizing the criminal behavior that got me locked up. You have to actively choose your lifestyle in prison because if money can buy it, anything can be available in the prison just like it is on the outside.

Nobody was sending me money and I couldn't get a job until the system processed me, so my only source of income for a while was bartering with other inmates and all I had to bargain with was food the prison gave me.

The prison didn't give us freebies, so to get basic things I needed – soap, toothpaste, deodorant – I would sell the food off my tray. If I needed envelopes to write people, all I ever got in return was being hungry because they never responded.

I turned that prison into my own personal rehabilitation center and I filled my days with any classes or group therapy they would let me into, even tried to find my way back to religion. There were mandatory programs that were assigned based on your record, like self-modification, behavior modifications, parental counselling, domestic violence; the prison library offered courses like computer classes and barbering classes.

Some guys had TVs, walk-mans, and stereos. All I had was the library and my classes. I was always reading a cookbook, or I was studying something. They would laugh at me because I walked around with my books. The other inmates used to talk shit to me, saying, "Man, fuck all that spiritual bullshit, you know you're going right back to the streets." Deep down, I knew that this was my last chance to turn my life around and I was trying my hardest at anything to get clean. The less free time I had, the better, because when I was idle, I was more likely to fall back into old temptations. More than that, it helped my reports and chances of parole because it showed that I was using my time to do something meaningful and that I was actively seeking a spirituality that would sustain me.

As hard as I tried to avoid anything that reminded me too much of my past, one guy, Fox, was from my hood and he knew all about my family, my glory days in the streets, and my history with addiction. Fox had beef with me because I wouldn't be part of the crew and was trying to fix the problems that had landed me in prison. He wouldn't leave me in peace to mind my own business.

One day, in the yard in front of everybody, Fox called out to me, "I hear your baby mama is expecting."

"That's good for her." She was working at the same prison I was at but I hadn't heard from her once since I had been locked up. I had no idea how my son was doing.

Fox moved closer and he said, "My homeboy knocked your baby mama up."

I pushed through the group to get to Fox, until it was like he was almost in my face. "What's your fucking problem with me, Dogg?"

In a moment of sincerity, he pulled me to the side and said low, "You making us look bad…saving your food out the chow hall like a squirrel."

I hated it as much but that was a matter of survival. Instead, I asked him, "She's dating another hood guy?"

"Nope," Fox said, "This time it's an inmate from the inside."

I was speechless. I couldn't believe she had fell for the banana in the tail pipe. I could understand another guard, somebody she worked with – all the free men in the world, and she dates a guy in prison?

Months later, Fox would shout across post 8, our cell block in prison, "7 pounds 4 oz baby girl, she had the baby!" Everyone knew, even the prison officials. She violated the law by having a relationship with a prisoner and ended up getting fired from the prison, with a brand new baby and no job. She never brought my son to visit me but still visits the prison because her new baby daddy was doing 25 to life.

After dinner we would be locked down in our dorms. Most of the guys hung out in groups, but mostly I'd be reading. This older guy, Morris, liked to play dominoes and once he saw me sitting by myself, he asked me to play with him. They would play for snacks from the commissary to eat late at night. He offered me some cookies; no strings attached. I didn't have any money and you know better than to take stuff from people because that's a favor, and even if they're offering, you don't take it 'cause there's something underlying with it. But he was friendly and the idea of trading the snacks for something I needed, or even maybe just eating them myself was tempting. So, I took it and played with him and some other old timers. For a little while, we became domino buddies every day after dinner.

One day Morris handed me three tapes. "I don't have a tape player," I said blankly.

"No," he laughed. "I see you trading your food! You gotta go sell the tapes! Go make you some money, get what you need."

He told me to go out on the yard and just ask around if anybody wants to buy a tape, but I felt so foolish, like I was a kid again, dragging Uncle Billy's lawn mower around the neighborhood. People in the world were using CDs and iPods and here I was, standing in the middle of the prison yard with three outdated cassette tapes.

A guy stopped me and asked if I was selling them – how much for all three? I didn't even know how much to sell them for. He saw I was confused and told me three tapes usually go for 15 bucks. We weren't allowed cash in prison, so he brought me 15 dollars' worth of stuff from the commissary: honey buns, cookies, candies, chips, deodorants. Whatever the value on the store list in the commissary – honey buns cost a dollar, soap cost 40 cent – that's the exchange value.

"That's yours!" he said, shaking his head when I brought it all back to Morris to share. "You're on your feet, go trade for more tapes and sell 'em again!" We got reshuffled from the same dorm not long after and I don't know what happened to him.

I asked everyone if they had any tapes for sale and I figured out pretty quick that I didn't even need to have the tape itself to sell it. Tapes have a little sleeve that has a description of the artist and songs – I told guys if you're selling a tape, you don't even have to give me the tape, just give me the sleeve or tell me the tracks and I'll match you up with someone and make sure everything is in good condition.

Communication has always been one of my strong points and I started me a middle-man exchange business, going from selling cassettes to selling everything. I had no products but I made a daily list of items people were selling and another list of things people wanted. I forged relationships and figured out the needs and wants of guys all over the prison and I mixed and matched supply and demand. Tapes, shoes, clothing, books, pictures, magazines, cigarettes, candy, cosmetics…everything. My cut was a dollar for small trades, 20 percent for bigger things. People trusted me and when they left the prison, they would even give me their things.

After a little while, I was self-sufficient and gone were the days of trading food for soap. The exchange business confirmed that I'm a good salesman and I knew I could make it legitimately. I just had to sell things that aren't illegal! Guys I knew were putting drugs in their butts and risking their freedom chasing the life that got them stuck in here. If you get caught with drugs in prison, they add another charge on top of what you did and you'd get a new sentence. A bubble gum wrapper of weed would get you 5 years extra and I didn't want to get caught up in that again! I had to turn the drug dealing light off to truly step away from the streets.

A riot broke out in the prison one afternoon and I found myself seeking safety in an office. I walked straight out of chaos but I ended up meeting the counsellor who just happened to be in charge of assigning jobs. While we waited for the ruckus to die down in the halls, I told her that I was a chef and about my experience and the next thing I knew, she had called me back into her office and gave me the job assignment of working in the kitchen. The counselor did tell me that giving me this job might get me killed, but I didn't take what she said for real.

On the first day I reported to work, the rest of the staff automatically assumed that I was there to wash dishes. Ms. Harris was in charge, a short white lady who looked wildly misplaced in the prison kitchen. She spotted me in the doorway and came out from the office, ushering me into the prep and cooking area. It looked like pretty much any other commercial kitchen I'd been in, except that the knives were attached to the prep tables by short chains and we made huge batches of everything in giant kettles, big enough for a man to fit into.

I literally watched the whispers that passed around the room as the rest of the men realized that I got the job – someone fresh off the street – and their stares changed from guarded curiosity to open hostility. If looks could kill, I would have been dead on the spot. A group of the men working in the kitchen approached me after our shift, backing me into a corner out of sight from any guards, and I found out that another prisoner had been waiting on that job for years. If I didn't quit, they threatened to kill me.

For the next few days, I continued to go to work, but I was constantly uneasy and moved with caution. It hadn't even occurred to me until I stepped foot in that kitchen but I realized that I needed this job to help keep me grounded and in touch with who I was on the outside. I wanted it as badly as I wanted to get clean but at this job feeding the prison population, I was only worth thirty cents an hour - and I knew that I didn't want to die for it.

I was walking down a hallway towards the kitchen when somebody called out my name. I kept moving because I didn't know if it was someone trying to attack in retaliation for taking and keeping the kitchen job. Even though I was ignoring it, the person kept calling my name and I had to find the source. I turned around and made eye contact with a guy with a chest like a barrel and arms so huge they looked like he could put me in a headlock and crush my skull with ease.

Momentarily I froze and then I felt a smile spread across my face for the first time in days as I recognized my cousin. In a different life, we had been thick as thieves, but I hadn't seen or spoken to him since before he went to prison almost 15 years prior. When we were kids, he was a scrawny thing, knobby knees and elbows, but he'd clearly been using his time and energy productively. He pulled me off to the side and we started talking as though we'd never spent any time apart.

Prison is a lonely experience and seeing each other gave us both a sense of relief: this was someone who knew me from before all of this. I filled him in on family gossip and finally I could share the burden of the death threats over my job in the kitchen with someone. My cousin had been in prison for years and he'd come up in the ranks and had connections in all the right places. He told me that I couldn't quit because working in the kitchen is a powerful position in a prison. They would make sure I was protected. I agreed because quitting wasn't an option.

I didn't know on my first day, but Ms. Harris had little professional kitchen experience and when I got the job, she was on the verge of losing hers. Using the skills I had learned at all of my past jobs, I showed her ways to become more efficient in kitchen management and made myself indispensable to her and we formed a type of alliance: Ms. Harris needed me to maintain her position and in return, she was willing to let me run things my way. After 2 years, she made me head cook, in charge of meals for over 1400 people.

I even got myself in good with the Warden and helped him secure quality suppliers by calling in some favors with buddies I knew from the restaurant business. The Warden went on a fishing trip once and I was called up to the front office during his absence. It was the Warden on the phone – he had caught a marlin, a very high-end fish and he wanted to ask if I knew how to cook it. A few days later he showed up at the prison with the marlin in a bag covered with ice. It was easily over a hundred pounds.

Even with the knife attached to the table by a chain, I wielded it like a scalpel and portioned and fileted that fish with surgical precision. The officers were amazed at my ease and speed and they joked about how they hoped nobody tried anything with me because they might end up in the next meal.

I cooked blackened marlin with mango salsa, fried plantain, and quinoa and the warden's front office was ecstatic. That was the first meal I had cooked or eaten in years that was made with fresh, fancy ingredients. If we'd made small portions, there would have been enough for all of the prisoners to get at least a tiny taste of the outside world, but they let me have a plate and then ate their fill, taking the leftovers home themselves.

I attended every single religious service and study group the prison offered. I needed the structure, the positive support and atmosphere. I hoped that religion might give me a spiritual edge and I needed to be certain to cover my ass, so I prayed to any and all Gods who would listen and attended meetings with every religious group, just in case God was on the other line, or had his phone off the hook, or had put me on hold when I called. My grandad was half Indian and I was even allowed to Tribe service.

They would light the smoke around me and wave the eagle feathers around my head.

I was raised in the Southern Baptist Church but a religion that I found in prison that gave me the sense of security and peace that I was searching for was Islam. Along with cooking, being in the fold of Islam with the Muslim brotherhood, reading the Koran, learning Arabic, and praying five times a day helped to support and discipline me.

Among my Muslim brothers was Duck, a man who looked like Bill Cosby with pop bottle glasses. He carried the title of Security in Arms, charged with holding the brethren accountable. Within our religion, Duck had the authority, the duty, and was well within his rights to publicly bring any of the brethren up on charges. Even though all of us were already prisoners, Brother Duck liked to say, "You were born out of law, you stay out of law, and my job is to put you in the law." Being out of law referred to doing something that was *Haram*, outside of Islamic beliefs. He was a recovering addict who had found self-worth in Islam – probably for the first time in his life – and along with it, power and authority.

I still maintained my middle man exchange business, so between that and my job as head cook, I no longer had to trade for basic necessities but I liked to sneak some food out of the kitchen after my shifts to eat later, despite it being strictly against the prison rules – stealing. As someone cooking the food, I didn't always get a chance to eat at the same time as everybody else and I'd get hungry long after mealtimes – and in my opinion, since I worked in the kitchen and cooked the food, I had a right to it anyway. I worked hard and did my best to make sure that the food going out to the rest of the prisoners tasted good. They remembered all too well what bland and mushy prison food tasted like under the last head cook and I had forged ties with men all over the prison.

In Islam, stealing is a cardinal sin, but Brother Duck was known to take a bribe and look the other way, especially when it came to the gay boys – there were rumors that he was a four-footed duck in the shower. I thought that if Duck benefited from my hustle, he wouldn't expose me and I always made sure to give him extra portions of food in the cafeteria and slip him snacks here and there after meetings. Between being in the Islamic fold and the protection from my cousin's crew, I was secure in that no other groups could touch me or force me to give them extra rations.

There was an Iman in our midst that I wanted to make a connection with because he was from Grand Rapids and I had plans to return there and build a foundation when I was released. I knew that he could be a good person to guide me in my transition. After our formal Friday congregational prayer, *Jumu'ah*, there would be a meeting and my hope was to introduce myself.

After our prayer, Duck took the floor and all attention was on the Security in Arms. I sat there anticipating my opportunity to connect with the Iman after the judicial review and when I heard Brother Duck begin to talk, his voice seemed like something far away in the distance. It became clearer when I heard my name fall from his lips. "Brother Wallace, we are bringing you up on charges. You are a good brother, you do your job, you study, you pray, you good with them white folks and they love you," he said, "But I'm bringing you up on charges because you like to steal."

I did a double take like a Looney Tune and zoned in. My state of perfect peace fled my body and I went into denial and defense mode. I admit the other brothers had warned me that Brother Duck was merciless and that he would get you, but I had not taken heed.

Sure, I had stolen food, but the very same Brother Duck who was bringing me up on charges had reaped the benefits of my offense. I'd assumed that by supplying Brother Duck with extra food, stolen or not, it would keep me from being charged. I tried to defend myself and said, "But Brother Duck, I shared the food that I took with you!"

His only response was that he was going along with it to see just how long I was going to be out of law. I was furious, more so for him exposing me in front of the Iman. Brother Duck had the power here, but I was the cook and it was apparent that he was willing to cut off his extra food supply for his duty. Like Elmer Fudd, I privately declared that it was Duck Season and right then and there, I vowed to hunt down that Duck.

The next day I observed Duck come into the chow hall. I wasn't a server, so my position was not on the line serving food. As the head cook, I had the authority to check on the line to monitor the food supply and see how the servers were doing. I rarely did, but this was my opportunity to flex my authority and exert some power.

As Brother Duck approached the server, I walked up to the server and told him to step aside. I dipped the serving spoon into the fries, picking up the same healthy portion which he had become accustomed to because of the VIP privileges I had given him. I reached forward, hovering the spoon for a moment over his tray and then with a flick of my wrist, I shook the spoon over him, showering him and the floor in fries. I made sure to maintain eye contact with Brother Duck and shook the spoon harder, causing the excess fries to fall. I looked down at the spoon and then back up at Brother Duck and I shook the spoon again and when I was done, there were only three or four fries remaining in the spoon. I extended the spoon and placed these fries on his tray.

He angrily challenged me, "You gonna do me like this?"

"You're holding up the line," I replied with a smirk and a simple shrug. The next server in line had already gotten out of my way and to add insult to injury, I grabbed the tongs and gave him the smallest piece of chicken I could find.

Indignantly, Duck refused to move, forcing me to call on Ms. Harris. She stepped up to the line and crossed her arms, irritated, barking, "Duck, you'll eat what you're given – now, get out of my line and stop holding everyone up!"

Duck was furious and even as he backed out of the line, he belted out "You want to go to war with me?" From that moment, it was on.

Over the next days, Ms. Harris stood side by side with me as I continued to trim Brother Duck's rations and watch him grow slim. She would shoo Duck and the few Muslim Brothers who sided with him away as they lay in wait outside the chow hall ready to seek revenge. In the end, he realized there was no beating me and gave up his crusade. He didn't want to continue starving and was trying to protect his ego and what little was left of his reputation. Eventually, he quietly let it go.

My war had been with Brother Duck, not the rest of my Muslim brothers and I found out much later from them that Brother Duck said he would see me conversing with the guards like we were good 'ole buddies, as if I wasn't even in prison. This was the root of Duck's being out to get me. Duck resented any privileges my job afforded me, was under the impression that I wasn't suffering or serving a sentence but that I was being celebrated. He said sarcastically that he wanted a pat on the head too.

What he saw as senseless celebration, I knew was calculated decision making on my part to get to where I was. Controlling food was controlling the prison and I was in control at every touchpoint.

The prison library was my school and my safe haven, a rare quiet corner of the prison where, for the most part, people let you be. I passed much of my free time in between the bookshelves reading and taking the classes they offered. I learned how to use a computer and surf the internet in there, on an old windows desktop with dial-up internet. The first time I sat in front of it, I didn't know where the on button was. It was like standing in front of a spaceship looking for the start button. The world was moving fast outside and here I was trying to keep up behind a barbed wire fence.

Sometimes, guys would take the cookbooks from the library and hide them from me because they all knew I wanted them. It would have been easier to just stick to the routine meals and even though I was limited by the ingredients and restrictions of the prison budget, I wanted to get as creative as I could and cook up different things. If I wanted to read the cookbooks, I had to rent it back from whoever took it; I paid in food I snuck out of the kitchen. That's how the rules were played. I didn't mind too much – I could've just shrugged and walked away, but all these locked up men were hungry and feeding people is what I do best.

I was good at reading and understanding and following all of the prison policies and procedures and thanks to the perks I received from my position as head cook, I never got myself in any serious trouble with the guards. But I was in prison for armed robbery and I knew that going to court with a court appointed attorney was going to get me nothing except back in front of a judge. So, I shifted gears and traded out cookbooks for legal books. I started spending my days in the prison library learning about the intricacies of case law so I could represent myself and fight my own case and I learned prison policies until I could recite them right out of my head. Knowledge is power and I realized that I could use what I had learned to help the other men inside.

I started a legal consulting service for the other prisoners and I was good at it. Word of mouth spread quick: men would come to me with their problems and I would conduct the research and help them write up grievances or respond to their charges, advise them on what to do and say during their hearings. Nothing serious: filing motions, filing for divorce, amending back child support, and my favorite, beating jail house tickets.

The Correctional Officers wrote tickets whenever they felt we stepped out of line – for being out of place, or talking back, or fighting. A ticket would take away any good time you had earned up and the officers held it over us as leverage to keep guys in prison. More often than not, the prisoners would just suffer the consequences, but I knew how to break down the tickets and find flaws, figured out that most of the CO's didn't care enough to write up the tickets properly or pay attention to the small technicalities. The hearing officials would not tolerate tickets that weren't written correctly.

I knew Jones would seek me out. My usual fee was just a 50-dollar store order in the commissary, but Jones was desperate and when he came to me with his case, he offered me his entire prison lifesavings —boom boxes, cassette tapes, shoes, clothes, and Penthouse magazines — if I could help get him out of it. I asked for the ticket and told him I would look it over and see what I could do. I had to gather all the jailhouse gossip before I took on his case. You can't take every case because guys would put their faith in you and if you couldn't get them out it would be hell to pay.

The guards knew all about my side hustle and started talking shit to me, taunting me, _I bet you want to beat Jones' ticket, Wallace, but we got his ass dead center._ I turned that ticket upside down but Correctional Officer Cunningham had Jones locked in over a barrel of wine and the evidence was hard to beat. Everyone was wondering how the hell I was going to beat that ticket. People were taking bets; in prison where entertainment choices were slim, they would bet on anything. He was sure to get the business from the parole board, but Jones wasn't worried about that – his real concern was his wife and mother threatening to cut him off if he didn't get a parole on his next hearing date.

There was only one trick left up my sleeve: it was my shift to clean the officers lounge and there it was pinned on the wall, the officers weekly schedule. Cunningham was off the day he wrote the ticket.

I had a grin on my face and as I walked past Jones pacing in the yard, I grabbed his arm to walk with him. In a low voice, I said, "Pack your shit, I got his ass." I told him the two questions to ask when he walked in the office: what day the ticket was written and what date Cunningham had off. Sometimes, in the heat of the moment, the CO's would forget to write up the ticket and not remember to do it until later and get the dates mixed up, invalidating the claim. Jones looked skeptical and nervous but calmly, I told him, "Trust me."

Rumor had even made it back to the guards that *Cunningham, Wallace got your ass.* As I walked past the officer station and Cunningham called me over, sneering "Let me get a pat down, Wallace," and giving me a lil' love tap in the process.

At the showdown on hearing day, I stood outside of the Hearing Investigators Office to find out the results. Jones showed with all he had but I refused to take even the usual retainer fee. I sent him in there like it was his first day of school but the bout didn't even last 2 minutes and Jones came out of there happy as hell.

Even when they didn't directly come to me and ask for help, I was inclined to step in if I saw the opportunity for a better outcome. The state of Michigan wouldn't allow guys to just sit around doing their time. If you didn't have some type of education, getting a GED was one of the conditions in order to be granted parole. This kid named Marcus couldn't obtain a GED – he'd seen the parole board three consecutive times with the same results: denial. I didn't know Marcus that well but I heard around the block that he had got flopped again by the board. I was almost positive I had the answer for him but I had to be able to get to him to talk.

He hung around a bunch of guys that protected him. They were from Chicago, Black Stones Rangers, the type who had a ritual when shaking hands that took like five minutes. When I approached, they pushed me away but I had to ask, even if it got me beat up – or killed. When I finally got through, he was sitting on his bed, head bent over the letter from the parole board.

He looked up at me. "What's up, hustle?"

I took a breath to steel my nerves and then asked, "Were you in special classes when you were in school?"

He stood up, crowding me into his friends. "Nigga, what the *fuck* is wrong with you?"

Holding my hands out to shield myself, I said, "Hold on man, I got something to show you."

"I don't want shit from you."

"No, no - read this," I protested, holding out a photocopy of a page from a law book in the prison library.

"Nigga are you trying to be funny?"

"Man, hear me out." By then I was surrounded by his troops. "I can get you out if you fall under these policies."

"What fucking policy?" he asked roughly.

With patience, I repeated, "Were you in special education when you were in school?"

"Yeah, man," Marcus crossed his arms over his chest. "Now what?"

"From which grade?"

He looked me up and down, eyes narrowed and then admitted, "All of them."

"What's the school's name?" I asked and then, "Can you get your people to call the school and get the school records?"

Nodding, Marcus said, "I can do you one better, you can call them right now," and he pulled a cellphone out from where he'd had it stashed. I was impressed for a moment and then I called straight through and had them mail me his school records.

Once I received his records, I wrote to the Parole Board on Marcus' behalf: Michigan case law states that if you have a learning disability you are not held to the requirement of obtaining a GED. Marcus had a pass coming because of the fact that he had dyslexia and it had never been made official on his prison records.

It took almost two weeks before Marcus heard anything back. I was walking on the yard coming from the library and I saw his boys coming straight for me, Marcus in the middle, his usual position. My heart skipped a few beats as the thought that I was about to get the beat down on the yard crossed my mind.

Then Marcus grabbed me and he exclaimed, "Man, your ass got me out of here! I'm going home next week!" I swear his eyes were extra shiny when he said, "All these niggas round here ain't doing nothing to help nobody… and you didn't even know me."

Standing outside of the room, I bounced on the balls of my feet, anxious for my first chance to go before the parole board. I had spent four years in prison trying to better myself, determined to prove to society that I was more than an addict and a drug dealer and I was confident that I was going to get out.

A guard ushered me inside and before I could even sit down at the parole board meeting, the head of the board told me, "I'll see you again next year, buddy." They hadn't even given me an opportunity to introduce myself.

Confused, I wondered what the purpose of this meeting was if they had already decided my fate. Somehow managing to keep my voice steady, I asked them to let me show them what I had done. They granted me half an hour to plead my case. After thirty minutes of sharing with them my life for the last four years, describing to them my accomplishments of getting clean, running the kitchen, and finding religion, I was still denied.

The head of the board stated that he could not sign his name granting my parole without me having taken the Assault Offender Program – which was at another prison and took a year to complete. I thought to myself, *where is this coming from?* I wasn't in prison for a violent crime. He explained that he and the board had to make sure that I was rehabilitated and upon reviewing my records saw that I had – in the past – displayed intimidating posture. My 'displays of intimidating posture' were the fights where Sky had called the cops on me and had been claimed by the lady in the bank. She hadn't even seen me take the money, but that was a better excuse than admitting she hadn't been paying attention at work and it was her word against mine.

The prison officials decided they couldn't take any chances and that I was going to be transferred to another prison to complete the Assault Offender Program. Based on the effort I put in and the progress that I made, I felt that I deserved to get out, believed that I had *already* earned it. My spirit was crushed. I worried so much that I lost one of my long glorious braids, forcing me to let my hair go. To earn my freedom, I had to trade off on the small comforts that I had worked so hard to establish, including the joy of my cooking and the privilege and prestige that it gave me and the occasional kisses and brushes against my body from a cute little female officer.

A guy I was friendly with came and helped put it all in perspective. He encouraged me to pull it together and to get back to my routine, helping me understand that the time of my release was not in my control. "Look around you," he told me. "There's men in here who are never going to get out. You still got a chance."

One of the requirements of the Assault Offender Program was to participate in group sessions, where everyone had to sit in a circle and listen to each other talk about their vices and what we had done to get here. We were supposed to question and challenge and express remorse for what we did to our victims. I reluctantly stated what my vice was in accordance to my paperwork, which was "intimidating posture". I didn't want to admit any violent behavior because the crime I got locked up for hadn't involved violence – in my eyes, my crimes were non-violent and had involved protecting myself when attacked and cussing my ex-wife.

What we were imprisoned up for wasn't a typical conversation topic and outside of the group sessions, it was generally better not to ask. During one session, this little guy, a self-proclaimed gangster rapper, recounted the night when he committed his crimes. He told us that he was looking for a ride and he hatched a plan to jack the car of the next people he saw. A church-going looking couple ended up being his victims – this guy approached them beside their car and then he shot the husband and the wife. He described to us that as he drove down Seven Mile, he heard a baby crying and realized it was coming from the backseat. Then, he pulled the car over, put the baby in the middle of the street and sped off.

Everyone in the group was silent and sat there speechless. One of the guys finally broke the silence, asking, "What kind of car was it for you to do that?" He replied that it was a Chevy Nova. He had killed two people in cold blood for *that*.

Although I had been in prison for years, during these group sessions was the first time that I truly realized what type of people I was around. After a year, the board granted me early parole. I was placed in a re-entry program, where we took classes on resume writing, participated in support groups, and were connected with resources that we would need when returning to the outside world.

2014 Washington D.C. Convention Center
Cooking Light Magazine promotion

2014 Miami, Florida
Morning News

2015 with Chef Paul
O'Shea at Montauk
Yacht Club

After Prison

2008-2009: MICHIGAN

After seven years, I had served my sentence and I was released from prison in the fall of 2008. I requested to be paroled to my oldest sister but somehow, God had other plans for me and I was at the mercy of the system. My paperwork was unclear of my destination – all I knew was that I was going to be dropped off somewhere on the east side of Detroit. Although it was only a little over an hour's drive away, my home in Lansing felt like it was on the other side of the world.

I had stayed with my Aunt Dean in Detroit as a youth. My Aunt Dean had 8 kids of her own but there was always room for one more. Her daughter, my cousin Lisa, had come to visit us in Lansing many years before when we were children. She saw what was happening to me and started to ask questions and I ended up confiding in her the horror story that I was living – getting beat, deprived, neglected, and emotionally assaulted. Lisa squeezed my hand hard and told me to catch the bus to Detroit, assuring me that Aunt Dean would let me stay.

I started plotting my escape shortly after Lisa returned to Detroit. I had a blow-out sale for all my customers, cutting grass for half price until I had saved up the bus fare to run away to Detroit. I arrived at the bus station and after buying the ticket all I had was a paper bag full of

"

clothing and seven dollars left over. Sometimes, I wonder how my life would have been different, if my mom had let me stay with my Auntie when I was 15.

Getting off the bus in the city to start a new life almost felt like it did all those years ago as a scrawny kid, except this time, as a grown man fresh out of prison, the world loomed around me, somehow bigger and more daunting. All I had were the two rubbers that the prison gave me as a 'care package' to newly released inmates and a few bucks to my name.

Only when I was on the way there, was I told that my destination was called SHAR House. Looking out the window at the world speeding by, I decided that's where God wanted me to be. I thought it might be a halfway house until I got there and saw a sign outside the building that read *Self Help Addiction Rehabilitation.*

Waiting in the lobby to sign paperwork and be admitted, the guy that was sitting next to me was accompanied by an older lady. They called his name and they both stood up and she stopped right dead center of him looked him square in the face, saying, "Baby, just do it for your mama. You love your mama." This grown man towering over her could barely nod his head as his lip trembled like it was his first day of school. In a sense, SHAR house taught grown folks how to be grown again, so it was a little like the first day at school of having a sober life.

When my name got called and it was my turn, I got up and walked into an office. The man behind the desk had a nametag that said *Elgin* and the first words that came out his mouth were, "What's your drug of choice, dope?"

I had gained some weight in muscle while I was locked up and I stood up like *nigga you about to get business.* It couldn't be the first time that he had seen that look: Elgin was a clever old-school cat and he knew how to maneuver around any situation. He said, "Hold on big fella, now you came to us." I was offended but I would come to learn that SHAR House was straight to the point.

I told him that there was clearly a miscommunication because I still had no idea what SHAR House actually was. He explained to me that this was an intensive drug treatment center and I corrected him, telling him I was a drug *dealer*, not a drug user. I was still in denial that my recreational drug habit of seven years was actually an addiction. I tried to get out of it, get them to send me somewhere else, but Elgin denied me on the grounds that according to my psychological report, I had hidden issues and the parole board had sent me to SHAR house to get me some help.

I was crushed with what I thought was another obstacle to face, not knowing that this one would be my savior. I was in complete denial and I was rebellious and I wanted to go home. I didn't do anything they said to, even though

I was obligated to attend five NA or AA meetings a day. Then, after being there for some time, in one day, two people came and did small things that ended up having huge impacts on the rest of my life.

Frank (brother-in-law of Jalen Rose, the sports analyst and NBA basketball player) who worked at Shar House, came into my room with some clothes and said, "Here you go," and dropped them on the bed. I only had one outfit, the prison khakis I was released in and I still wore those every day. People are not defined by the clothes they wear but they do directly impact how people see you and how you see yourself. I was in disbelief. It was nice stuff too and wearing it made me feel more like myself than I had in a long time, which cheered me up enough that I began to mingle around a little bit.

The staff noticed the shift in my behavior and later that day, this wonderful lady allowed me to use the phone to talk to my family. After I hung up, she told me, "You would get more out of being here if you participated in the program and stopped being so nasty to everyone." Softening her tone, she said, "I wasn't trying to eavesdrop on your conversation but I heard about you talking to your auntie about cooking and we sure could use your help in the kitchen. Our cook is out sick."

She put me to work that same day and once I got in the kitchen, I realized how much I missed it and I was focused like never before. I took control and reorganized everything, adding structure to the kitchen, the workers, how they ordered the food. The food here was different.

It was all donation based. I was feeding 200 people rather than the 1200 in prison. I was throwing down. I had to show people that I wasn't no dummy. I had a lot of purpose in this life.

Soon, I became a trusted person at the treatment center and eventually I was even doing intake on the late-night shifts after the staff would go home. I enrolled into the extended day program where they helped with housing and numerous other resources and the 90 days turned quickly into 6 months. I was there long enough that they kept entrusting me with more and more responsibilities, like helping new admissions through intake. I started seeing the people coming through that really needed help. I understood that SHAR House was really helping people overcome addictions – from alcohol to heroin to crack to meth. It made me want to approach my life with new purpose.

A guy came in one day and he was dressed nice, a factory worker from the auto plant. When he had low work performance, he was subjected to a random drug test, which he failed. It was either SHAR House or lose the job – and SHAR House was a good choice. Before I came to SHAR House, I had no experience dealing with heroin. Even the lingo was foreign to me. During intake, he kept saying to me with such desperation in his voice, "Someone is going to have be with me when I get sick."

He kept saying he was going to get sick, over and over again.

At night before all the staff had left for the night, everybody kept giving me all this contact information and saying, "Tee, you gonna have a rough night with this. Call if it gets out of hand."

Naively, I didn't know how serious they were. Around midnight that night, some other guys staying in the home came to my room, saying, "He's sick and saying he's going to leave and go get a blow." I went to find him and he was rocking back and forth, moaning the word *sick* to himself over and over. Knowing it wasn't enough, I offered him, "You want a Tylenol? I can't give you anything stronger."

He groaned, "Man, what the fuck are you talking about, I need a blow."

I barely knew what he was talking about and eventually in a small voice he said, "If you stay here with me, I can kick it," and so I did. I sat with him for hours and held his hand and did my best to comfort him. That man trembled and shook like a leaf and it got so bad he was throwing up and shitting on himself at the same and all I could do was try to clean him up as best as I could.

That night, I gained a new understanding about drugs and the havoc they wreak on people's lives and from that day forward, I never considered selling drugs again. When I left SHAR house, Elgin said to me casually, "A monkey can't sell bananas." I looked at him and he continued, "A monkey can't sell bananas because he will eat them all up."

Since I had arrived from the prison, I had not left SHAR House to see the outside world. It took some time to adjust to being out of prison but when I felt ready to start venturing into the world again, my friend Gloria asked if I wanted to come with her. Gloria was an ex-addict as well and she had turned her life around and committed her life to helping others. I met her at SHAR House, where she worked part-time and part-time for the Detroit Outreach Substance Abuse Program, a program that helped people in the urban community with obtaining basic supplies. I would ride with her to pass out supplies: soap, water, toiletries, toothpaste, food. We would go out and try to get people in treatment and sometimes, we even handed out clean needles, hopefully to at least alleviate addicts from spreading diseases.

They said if you came to Detroit addicted to drugs from another state, you would be dead in a year, because the drugs were twice as strong and twice as cheap. The things I saw in Detroit were heart wrenching and breath taking. The drug dealers were mixing heroin with this new drug called fentanyl so they could sell more of it and it made the heroin stronger. People were dropping dead like flies. The police were so frantic to get it off the streets they were trying to buy the drugs straight from the drug dealer.

I saw firsthand how this super heroin affected people at SHAR House. I remember meeting Allen Bray, the co-founder of Shar House. In a way, he and the program he created saved my life. This was the first and last time that I had ever met him. He was giving a speech before he went to have a heart transplant and he died from complications not long after. I remember seeing the staff at full attention. He gave a warning speech about the heroin addiction and how heroin was in his day and what heroin is now. From that day forward, I didn't want to be like anybody else, I didn't want to imitate another drug dealer, another basketball player, another entertainer. The person who I wanted to be, who has motivated me to this day, was Allen Bray. I felt, not for the first time in my life, that I wanted to be an advocate to help people. I didn't know how I could do it. How could I show my support?

I said as much to Gloria when we were packing up the van before we went driving around. She turned her head and looked me square in the eye "Terry, you really don't even know the skillset that you have. I'm only limited to this area right here," she said, pointing at the flat top grill in the back. We hooked it up to the back of the van sometimes and we'd drive somewhere and cook and pass out food. "I've seen you work that flat top grill and I seen the happiness that you bring to people with your food. You make people smile when you cook. You bring warmth and you bring comfort. You can go anywhere in the world and help people."

With a thoughtful look on her face, she told me to hook the grill up to the van. "I gotta run to the store," she said. "After that, we're going to Jurassic Park."

While I waited for her to return, I asked some of the guys who were with me in the Substance Abuse Program about Jurassic Park. I watched faces flicker in recognition and some even put their head down like the memories were painful. "It used to be a nice park," one of guys told me. "But people stay there and live in the woods until someone comes and pulls them out. People go there and never come out the same. It's called Jurassic Park 'cause anything and everything goes on in there."

I noticed that there was an ambulance already on location when we pulled up to Jurassic Park. People had placed flowers and cards at the entrance of the park and I realized they were memorials for people who had overdosed there. The park was lifeless, the grass was dry and patchy, with weeds sprouting everywhere. There were no rims on the basketball court, the seats were missing from the swing set and you could hear the chains rattling back and forth, like a sound effect from a horror movie. There were no kids in sight to play in the park, but that was a blessing because syringes and needles, empty crack valves, empty lighters and dime bags lay all over the ground.

As we unpacked the van, I said to Gloria, "What do you want me to do? It seems that you need to call the coroner instead of bringing a barbecue grill."

She rolled her eyes at me. "Terry, quit cracking jokes and fire up the grill."

I start cooking the bacon, cooking the sausages, cooking smothered potatoes with onions. The smokey smell of sizzling meat was dancing in the air and blew through the park, making the bushes rustle. But the park was empty and I said to her, "Nobody's here."

"There, in there." She smiled a little, gesturing with her head towards the overgrown woods. "They will come out."

I stood there watching and people started to appear from between the trees. For a moment it felt like seeing the music video for Thriller for the first time. They were all thin, ragged looking people, dirty with dark rings around their eyes, both women and men, addicts who were living out in the woods. The ambulance had pulled up and the paramedics pulled up and they started administering first aid to people who needed it. Gloria was talking to them, trying to get them into treatment, and I was doing what I do best: serving food. We passed out food to all of them and I made sure that anybody who wanted seconds, got them.

My attention landed on this one white kid, who looked old past his age, like he had put on extra years. He looked distressed and I heaped an extra big helping of food on his plate. "Don't you want to see your family? Don't you want to see your mom and your dad?" I said, "Come with me to SHAR House and they can help you get treatment." He stood by me the whole time as I was feeding people and even offered to help, but I told him that we needed somebody that was a little bit cleaner to pass out food. So, he sat at a bench watching me the whole time and never moved.

We fed everybody, probably around a hundred or so people and I watched a smile cross the face of every single one of them with some warm food in their bellies. That kid was the only one to come with us, but getting even one person into treatment out of a hundred was a victory. When we got him in the van, he smelled so bad we had to roll down the windows. At SHAR House, they took him to detox and then I didn't see him for a while. A couple of weeks after, I started noticing this new guy in the home – then he walked up to me and began to thank me for getting him into treatment. I figured out it was the same kid we pulled out of the woods and the change in him was like night and day. He told me that he was a law student who had lost his way in Jurassic Park and that his parents had come to visit him. He said that me and that flat top grill had saved his life. I still ride around city to city feeding people in need but with a bigger flat top grill in my food trailer.

The contrast between what I saw and experienced in the streets and many of the establishments where I worked was a stark and sometimes unsettling reality that was only sharpened as I readjusted to life outside of prison. The first place that offered me a job after SHAR House was the Detroit Yacht Club, located on the 982-acre Belle Isle Island on the river in between Detroit and Windsor and with just one bridge to Detroit, the island required a pass to access.

The staff warned me about people getting robbed while walking from the island at night. On my way home from work one night, I began to see what looked like small spots of light in the bushes and then I began to hear movement. I kept my pace and continued to walk, but I felt my heartbeat racing as I saw about five guys smoking cigars emerge from behind the trees.

I was sure that their intent was to rob me, but as they began to surround me, I offered them the only thing I had: food from the Yacht Club. Like the feeding of the multitude in the Bible, my dinner was shared between them and they became different as they ate, as they tasted and talked and exclaimed over how good it was. I saw in their faces how young they were and the understanding of the desperation they felt to lie in wait on this bridge to prey on people passing by wrenched my heart. The fear that gripped me as they approached melted away and was replaced instead by purpose and resolve, to help myself so I could help people like them.

One of those homeless guys asked me my name and I told him, "It's Tee." He nodded, and answered back with "Chef Tee," and that is how I got to be known as Chef Tee.

At most of the establishments where I worked throughout my life, I would always have a food allowance, meaning that we'd get discounts or free meals on the days we were working shifts. These allowances were one of the major benefits of my employment and meant that even when I was struggling, I was eating good.

My youngest sister would show up at the restaurant trying to take advantage of my food allowance and eat free. If she came alone, I would send her away and cuss her out, but she figured out that if she showed up with her hoochie momma friends and introduced me as her brother, the chef, she would be spared the humiliation. Her friends would eat modestly, but she would order a bunch of over-the-top, expensive items, wrecking my whole food allowance for the month.

One day she called me at work and I made the mistake of mentioning to her that her favorite singer Brian McKnight was staying in the hotel where I was working. When I got off work, I walked through the hotel lobby to find her sitting there, hoping that Brian McKnight would walk through the front doors. As luck would have it, as I walked towards her, Brian McKnight was also entering the lobby and she sprang into action. When she approached him and asked him for his autograph, he responded that he didn't sign autographs and upon hearing that, her eyes lit up like a deer. I immediately became very tense because I knew my baby sister. Brian McKnight didn't, but I did, so I knew what was coming. "Brian McKnight, how dare you?" in a high-pitched voice, she said, "I will call the radio station, I'm your number one fan and by us buying your records, we support your broke ass. It's your job to sign autographs." She was on stage doing a solo performance and Brian McKnight and his entourage were the audience. I left her there in mid performance, put my head down and made a beeline though the lobby towards my car. Security quickly escorted her out the hotel and I had to endure hearing how I was a punk all the way home because I didn't help her fight and how that was a shit hotel and lastly, don't wear that uniform in my house no more or you'll be walking to work.

Willie Earl, my former step-father, even showed up unannounced with his new family on Easter. He had on his best Salvation Army drop box, top ten pick suit and he was accompanied by his white wife, Tina, and their daughter. All the time when we were growing up, he would talk shit about the white man this and the white man that. I was convinced that he was a black power militant to the tenth power so when he married Tina I was confused. I unapologetically started questioning him; I reminded him of his verbal sermons against the white man and asked him why he had married a white woman, he responded, "Just to spite the white man".

Shug would refer to the new couple as Kermit the Frog and Miss Piggy and would relentlessly seek them out all over town and create a scene by publicly cussing them out.

She sent Tina fleeing the scene and running to the car in tears more than once with Willie Earl shortly tagging behind.

On those occasions, when she caught wind of them sunbathing from her informer, she would ride past their apartment as Tina was lying out on the complex lawn in a leopard bikini accompanied by Willie Earl who was wearing a straw hat and Bermuda swim trunks. My mom would ride by relentlessly taunting Willie Earl screaming that he looked like a melted Snicker bar lying beside a marshmallow and telling them they were the perfect couple because together they made a smore's bar. My mother was hell on the yard.

I was in the back cooking and I was told by the wait staff that my Dad was out in the dining area with his family. I was a bit confused because I didn't have a father in my life. Low and behold, when I entered the dining area, there was Willie Earl just bragging "Terry, my son!" and ranting and raving about me. The staff was feeding into it and saying to me "Your father this…and your father that". I was amazed and in so much astonishment that I was at a lack for words. It was Easter and I had mouths to feed so I just returned to the back and let him do what he was doing. I left him there, caught in another one of his delusions of grandeur which was so reminiscent of his secret world of play money and business plans.

2010: ALABAMA

The question that I get asked to me who know of me and my life was, how did you do it? How did you turn your whole life around? The truth is that changes were not made overnight. There was trial and error, relapse after relapse, and in between all of this there was self-evaluation. But before I could even begin to address my addictions, I had to recognize that I had a problem that was beyond my control.

Detroit was dangerous. All the parking lots were surrounded by barbed wire fences. Even in the McDonald's, everything was bulletproof glass. The Dollar Hit House was a place where you buy a hit of crack for a dollar: there was a slot you stuck your head through with two guys standing on the other side of. One of the guys would have a Louisville Slugger and the other would have a crack pipe with a lighter. So, you would stick your head inside this hole and they would tell you to pull on the pipe and if you kept pulling after the guy told you to stop, they would tap you on top of the head with the bat. I was starting to feel the urge to use again but I couldn't imagine being that desperate or getting that strung out and it scared me. Against the regulations of my parole board, I skipped town without their permission.

I left Michigan and went back to Alabama. I was just wanting to see my family and most of my siblings had returned south. I realized that I had to get back to him, to the kid that was nurtured, raised by, and belonged to Arlene and Neal Wallace, Thelma, and Jimmy. I had to get back to who he had been at his essence, at his core, which was a pure and good-hearted person. The streets of Michigan changed me: I had become a hardcore slickster, cunning, and manipulative. I had turned into a character that they only read about, a monster from horror stories, a nightmare come true. I had to pay attention to the monster and in this fight, I was trying to beat my worst adversary: I had to battle with myself.

It was a day-by-day process. It took time to become a monster and it would take time for me to regain myself. Your addiction is not the drugs. The core issues are within yourself and they have to be resolved. Most of the time, we self-medicate to hide the pain. As addicts, we need to address those issues in order to heal. I had to identify my triggers -- what set me off? In order to go right, I had to think about what made me go left: Who was around? What was I thinking? Who was I with that made me upset?

The first thing I did was to step outside of myself and look at the good, the bad, and the ugly. I wrote down 10 things I liked about myself and 10 things that I didn't like about myself and 10 things that were very ugly. In prison, my days were filled with all the self-help programs I could, from Anger Management to Narcotics Anonymous. Even though back then, I was still in denial over my own addiction, I was filling my arsenal with tools for readjustment and transitioning back to reality. I started going to NA and AA meetings again and the 12 steps of Narcotics and Alcoholics Anonymous guided me through the sources of my issues.

When I had first arrived in Alabama, one of my sisters greeted me and said, "I'm glad you're here. I just couldn't wait for you to get out."

I was glad to see her too, but I was still stuck. "Why didn't you visit me?" I asked. "Or why couldn't you send me any money while I was in prison?"

She rolled her eyes at me. "I don't have no money you know, I got two kids." Instead of apologizing, she said, "I told some guys I know about you and they gonna look out for you. So, I'm gonna take you shopping so you can look good for them."

The next day, a couple of guys came and picked me up and she told me to go for a ride with them. "I heard you're on the hustle. You sell dope real fast and you know how to cook it up." They offered me a modest amount of drugs and would come back and get the money from me.

When I got out of the car, my sister asked how it went. I realized she was setting me up for job interviews with drug dealers. A couple of other guys came and she kept asking what they say, what they say. I kept telling her they would get back with me. I went along on these rides with them talking the drug talk. But that wasn't my thing. I wanted nothing to do with my past, all I wanted to do was cook. Eventually she found out that I had actually been telling the drug dealers that I would get back in contact with them.

"Why you ain't got no work?" she demanded one day.

"You know I'm not trying to sell drugs anymore."

"How am I going to get my money back for the clothes that I bought you?" She didn't acknowledge what I had actually told her.

"Well," I said pointedly. "I'm going to get a job cooking."

"Terry, ain't nobody got time for that bullshit that you learned in prison. You need to get on your feet and I done hooked you up. I want my money back."

"What?" I asked blankly. "I thought you bought me the clothes just to help me out."

Her voice serious, she told me, "No, I bought you the clothes so you can look like you a drug dealer again."

I was no longer familiar with Birmingham. I had been gone a long time. I had been calling my sister up all week asking her to take me to the different restaurants around town. She took me to Chile's.

"What are we doing here?"

She said, "Well, you wanted a cook job."

I shook my head at her. "I'm a chef…"

"How you become a chef in prison?"

"Well, you just don't understand." I shook my head at her again and then asked her to take me to this country club.

She was kind of amazed at the property. "You gonna ask for a job washing dishes here?" she asked. I didn't even dignify her with an answer.

I went inside with my resumes in my hand. I went in and talked to the chef for a short while and he agreed to hire me part-time. When I went to the car, I didn't tell her I got that job. Instead, I told her to take me to a hotel downtown. I went inside and she sat in the car for about 40 minutes. "Now I got two jobs," I told her when I came back out. "I don't want to get caught up in all that slick shit you doing."

"You got two jobs?" she repeated back at me dumbly.

"One pays me $20 an hour and one pays me $18. I told you that I had learned how to cook."

"And they believe you?" she asked, instead of congratulating my victory.

Sky called me, out of the blue one day and told me, "Your son needs to be around you."

We hadn't spoken in a long time. I hadn't had contact with Sky or my son in years. "I'm staying with my mom in Alabama," I told her.

"He really needs to come to you," she said. "Otherwise, he's going to the juvenile detention center."

I wasn't in a position to either agree or disagree, so she sent him to Alabama where I was staying with Shug. When he saw me, he exclaimed, "Dad!" and my heart swelled because I hadn't seen him in 7 years, but he still knew who I was.

He didn't have much clothing with him, but he arrived just in time for me to get my first paycheck. My sister came over, but she was more interested in getting her money back than meeting her nephew.

"Can I give you half now, half after I get paid next time?" I asked mildly. "It's 'cause Terry's here and he don't have any clothes and I want to buy him some."

"I don't give a damn," she said stubbornly. "I want all my money right now for the clothes that I bought you."

I could be more stubborn than her. "I'm just gonna give you half of it," I insisted, but she was as petty as she was stubborn and she decided to get Shug involved.

My mom was like, "You know he's wanted in Michigan anyway, he left without permission. We'll call the police on him. I'm not gonna put up with Terry's shit." I heard them calling the cops on me. They told them that I was a fugitive from Michigan. That I was a bank robber. They called the police on me because they got mad I wouldn't fall in line with their demands like I used to and gave me no other choice but to flee with my son.

I went to my aunt's house and stayed over there for a few minutes. But I knew the police were going to be looking for us and we slipped out the back door so we could try to make our way out. The Federal Marshalls start surrounding the neighborhood looking for me and eventually tracked me to my sister's house. They bust in and put everybody on the floor. Junior and I were hiding in the closet.

The absconding team was called and they escorted me back to Michigan. I started my trip from Alabama to Houston. Then to New Mexico, Kentucky, Illinois. It took about 2 weeks of me riding handcuffed in a bus. All these inmates from all over the United States who had left without permission from their parole officers were being picked up. During this time, Junior stayed at my sister's house before his mother took him back.

Shug wrote the parole board a letter and told them that I was going to kill her if they let me come back to Alabama. They took me to a maximum-security prison for allegedly threatening my mom. She tried to use the system to her advantage to keep me in prison. If it weren't for my aunts and my other sister to tell them the truth of what happened, I might still be in there.

When I finally went in front of the parole board, they told me I had to go through a re-entry program. I got to pick a state where I wanted to go, I just couldn't go back to Alabama. During that parole board hearing, I made the decision to commit to participate in the programs. I had to be honest with myself, realizing that if I went back around my old stomping grounds in Lansing, I was likely to relapse. Grand Rapids was a new start, a clean slate.

2011: GRAND RAPIDS

My son was in foster care while I waited for my parole hearing. Sky had taken him back but she was also being investigated by the state for a relationship with another prisoner. She eventually lost all her kids for this reason. When I got to Grand Rapids, I wasn't even out of the halfway house a month-and-a-half before they gave me custody of my son.

Sky was trying to give custody of my son to her mother. I had no lawyer of my own, but I had learned enough helping other inmates in the legal library at the prison. "Excuse me, your honor," I said when I went to the court for the custody hearing. "I haven't lost my parental rights. I haven't done anything to violate the court system."

"Yes, Mr. Wallace, that sounds about right," the Judge intoned, "But we want you to get some parenting counseling classes."

"Your honor, I did," I said, holding up a folder of certificates, "I do have it. I took those classes while I was in prison."

Sky butted in, upset, "Well, he owes me $20,000 in child support!"

"You can't charge me for child support while I was in prison!" I protested. "I would like an audit on my child support. I was in the house with Miss Sky while she was receiving benefits from the state and I was giving her money as well." The judge asked for proof and I pulled out the probation papers with her at the same address. Sky got quiet, her cheeks red as he suspended all the child support. "Your honor, what about the child support that she should be paying me?"

That's when she exploded. "You want *me* to pay *you* child support?"

If I had to do it, why shouldn't she? The judge seemed to agree with me and he ordered her to pay the same as I had. "Excuse me, your honor," I said again. "I don't think that's right. She makes $100,000 a year and I only made $32,000 a year. How can her child support be the same as mine?" The judge recalculated her payments and her monthly payments ended up being twice as much as mine.

When I went to Grand Rapids, I was dropped off at a halfway house. Everywhere else – Lansing, Detroit, Alabama – I had people to turn to or people to drag me back down, but Grand Rapids was different. I didn't know anyone and I had nothing but my son, my prison uniform, and my prison boots. The clothes that were given to me, I sold, so that I would have enough money for bus fare and enough to make copies of my resume.

I went to pick my son up when he came out of Juvenile Court. He had all these fake gold chains around his neck, his pants were sagging off his butt, like he was trying to impress me with some faux swagger. In prison, I was always trying to encourage young men to dress appropriately and not walk around with their pants sagging off their butt. Little did I know it, my son would be my worst nightmare. My God, everything that I had hoped to never see in my son appeared as a result of the neglect from me being in prison. I stripped him down of all that and made him pull his pants up. But rap music and the idea of the streets had taken hold of my son. He dreamed of being a rapper. That was all he wanted to do. There was no doctor, no lawyer, he didn't want to do nothing else. All he talked about was, "Dad, when you going to teach me how to sell drugs?" He had an outdated image of me embedded in his head and I think that's why we didn't get along, almost to this day, because I had evolved without him.

While living in the halfway house, I met a man, Pimp, who would become my best friend, and as the years went by, he also became my brother. Pimp was also a drug dealer and was undergoing this alternative program similar to mine. He had the choice of this program or jail. He was a quiet man from Atlanta with a very similar background as mine. I had Junior with me this time but nowhere for us both to stay, as the halfway house didn't allow children. Junior was 11 by this time and I told the judge I had a house, when in reality I didn't. For two weeks, until I could afford a hotel room, Pimp helped me hide Junior in the halfway house until I could finally get a hotel room for us. All the guys in the program helped me in hiding Junior.

I looked up all of the programs that were affiliated with Michigan Rehabilitation Reentry Services that assisted with housing, work, tools, and transportation. These were programs in Michigan that were willing to help people who just got out of prison, but you had to be willing to follow their specific guidelines and most guys didn't want to do that. But the consequences of choices that I made were forcing Junior to grow up fast because we were in a city with no family and no safety net. I needed and wanted the help and so I went along with what the programs required me to do. I had to get signatures of places that I went to look for a job or for interviews. I would kindly ask them to sign and because of my willingness to do that, people were more than willing to help and sign what I needed.

When I got hired, one of the chefs working in the kitchen saw my prison boots and immediately identified me. He asked, "When did you get out?" and I felt my heart pound, fearful that he would become mistrustful of me. Instead, he said, "At least you got a job, my brother just got out and he already gone right back to prison."

Eventually, housing came through for me and Junior, and we moved into an apartment with only the sheets, blanket, pillows, and towels that we took from the motel.

Things were going good in Grand Rapids. I had Junior and I was going to counselling with him. One of the therapists informed me that my son was lonely and missing his mom. She suggested that I start dating and looking for a woman to bring into his life because he was missing a mother figure. When I asked him about it, he told me that he missed his mom.

I was at work one day and I saw these two black girls come in. It was unusual for black people to come into these upscale restaurants. It was an open kitchen and I waved at them from behind the counter. They giggled and waved back and called me over to their table. It was obvious they were not Americans because when they spoke, they had accents. When I asked, they told me they were African. One didn't look so hot and she was aggressive. But the other one was pretty, and very quiet, and I managed to get her number. Her name was Om Foo Foo.

We started hanging out, but it was always Om Foo Foo inviting me to the house she lived in with the not so hot looking girl. I was always telling her I would take her places, but it was like she couldn't leave. As we became closer, I shared what the counsellor had told me about my son needing a mother figure and we started talking about the possibility of marriage. I thought about my son and how I wanted to settle down for him to have the best life. I thought about how she wasn't from the hood and she wasn't okay with me running the streets, selling drugs. This was the closest I had been to living a normal, productive life.

It felt like a shotgun wedding, everything was planned at the last moment. We got married at the courthouse. I told Junior one morning that he wouldn't be going to school because I was going to get married today! We went out to the mall and stopped at the little jewelry shop. I only had $300, but she really didn't care what kind of ring she got, as long as she got something. I told her that I didn't have anybody to stand in on my behalf. A bunch of her African friends came and stood with her, people I didn't even know and had never met.

Junior kept saying, "Don't do it, Dad," even when we were standing in front of the judge, but I ignored his better sense and I went ahead and got married to her. I went to work that same night that I got married and I kept looking at my finger and rubbing the ring around it in disbelief.

She fell out with the girl she was working for, but because she had been a caretaker inside the home, Om Foo Foo knew all this medical terminology. "I can get you a job at the hospital," I promised her. "I know somebody."

I hooked her up with an interview with my friend, but afterwards, he called me up and said, "You know we can't hire people that don't have social security numbers."

"What do you mean?" I asked dumbly.

"Your wife doesn't have a Social Security number. She's here illegally."

As soon as she came home, I started asking Om Foo Foo questions about her status in the United States. She was silent for a moment, then all of a sudden the truth came pouring out of her. Om Foo Foo was basically a slave to the other girl. She came to the US on a student visa and did not return back to Africa when she was supposed to and so she worked for the other girl in her house as an undocumented worker. I was naïve and didn't know that foreign girls would try to get American guys to marry them for the green card. The guys from work had all questioned that I married a girl from Africa, but I didn't know that she wasn't legal. I really didn't realize that she was trying to gain citizenship. I hadn't been hunting her – she was hunting me. But I don't think Om Foo Foo did her research. She had no understanding of what marrying a guy who was on parole entailed: that I did not have the rights of a citizen and that I couldn't sponsor her citizenship.

One day I came home and these two little girls were there. She told me they were her god kids, but the girls kept calling her mama, mama, mama. She finally admitted that they were hers, and it all became too much. We separated.

Willie Earl died suddenly, and so my brothers and sisters and the entire family came to Michigan for the funeral to wish him a farewell to hell. Many of them I hadn't seen in years, since before I went to prison. I only had like one month left on parole and my sister convinced me that it would be a good idea to move back to Alabama because my son needed to be around his cousins.

I called Om Foo Foo so that we could meet. We hadn't seen each other in four months and she came to my place with ideas of reconciliation and hopes that I was going to go ahead with signing the papers for her to stay in the United States. Instead, I told her that I was moving to Alabama and that I wanted a divorce. "Why would you do something like that?" she demanded, determined to raise hell. "They are going to deport me! Do you want to send me back to Africa? You are an evil man. You black Americans don't help your own African people."

A little while after she left, someone pounded on my front door and when I opened it, two police officers were on the other side. "Mr. Wallace, you're on parole and you put your wife out of your apartment."

I opened the door to my apartment wider. "She doesn't live here – I haven't even seen her in 5 months before today! My name is on the lease, you can check!"

"What did you tell her?" they asked. "She's very distressed."

"I told her I wasn't signing papers for her to stay in the United States."

"Did you cuss at her?" I told them I did and one of them stepped forward, saying, "Well, sir, that's domestic violence, the third."

They took me to jail for a parole violation with one month left on a two-year parole. So, I'm sitting in the county jail and I'm thinking I didn't touch her, I didn't do anything. This is going to blow over, they can't do too much.

I had violated the terms of my parole and I ended up going back to prison for two years. It was 18 months that I did all together. They sent me back to prison at the Lakeland Correctional Facility. I sat in a prison for parole violators.

They had a culinary program there and I started to long for cooking again. I wrote a message on a prison kite to Chef Hill, the prison's culinary director and promised him that if he let me join the program, I would be more of a help than a hindrance. Pretty much my entire resume was outlined on that prison kite.

To my surprise, Chef Hill called me over to his class. He was a black man, real laid-back and smooth. "Which class are you here for?"

I said, "I'm in here for the domestic violence class."

He asked what happened and I described the situation with Om Foo Foo. "Y'all guys get out there not even off parole and get with these women and get jammed up," he shook his head and gave an exasperated sigh. "I have seen so many of you guys come back into prison because you get involved in a relationship and when it goes left, the woman knows you're on parole and calls the cops on you."

Then he asked, "You worked for Michigan State Kellogg Center? Who do you know?" I started naming some chefs I had worked under, like Chef Rajeev and he reached over and grabbed a photograph to show me. "Which one of these is Chef Rajeev?" I pointed at one of the men in the picture.

"I want you to cook something for my class," Chef Hill said. "Demonstrate what you got."

I had spent eight months in the county jail trying to fight the case before they sent me back to prison and it had been close to a year since I had stepped foot in anything resembling a professional kitchen. I whipped up a simple but tasty shrimp dish and I could see on his face that Chef Hill was impressed. "Man, that's pretty good," he nodded approvingly.

The cooking classes were offered once in the morning and once in the afternoon – you were only supposed to go to one or the other, but I made a point out of going to all of them. I soaked up all the information I could like a sponge, reading every single book cover to cover and watching all the videos in class with rapt attention. Chef Hill was bringing me extra material to learn from the outside world dealing with restaurant and hospitality management. I thought I already knew what it was, but I learned the real chef part of cheffing while I was locked up in prison.

Even though I was away from my son and I had violated my parole and I was back in prison, I was truly getting the most out of my cooking. I got two visits the whole time that I was in prison. Chef Rajeev came to see me. I was ashamed but I was happy and he told me that I had so much talent that I shouldn't be coming in and out of prison. I locked in and I studied hard every day.

Om Foo Foo came to the prison to see me and she told me that she would tell the parole board the truth if I did not divorce her for three years so she could continue to stay in the United States and file for citizenship. I agreed to the terms in exchange for her to write a letter telling what happened in the actual events of that day and submitted to the parole board. Once she submitted the letter and she took a sworn affidavit stating that she was telling the truth, I was released from prison.

2012: FLORIDA

My youngest sister knew that I was eager and bored. She was moving to Florida with her boyfriend and their two children and she asked me if I wanted to join them. Going there, we were all crammed snug into our only form of transportation, the U-Haul that my sister had talked somebody into renting her for the move. Since none of us had a car, she decided to hang on to that U-Haul for not even just a few extra days, but additional months. We stayed with some of her friends, a couple who lived in South Beach – my sister's family of four, plus me, cramming seven people into a small space for two.

I was eager to find work, so the next day I got on the bus with about twenty-five resumes in hand and a plan to drop them off at each hotel or restaurant along the five blocks. I made my way down the strip, starting at the Ritz Carlton as soon as I got off the bus. I hadn't even made it halfway down and I already had what felt like ten different job offers.

My sole purpose for going to Florida was for a new start and I wanted as much work as I could possibly handle because if I stayed busy working, I wouldn't slip back into using drugs. When I returned to the house where we were staying, I announced that I had 10 job offers and had to make a decision. I decided that I would take the

Ritz Carlton's offer and work it during the day and The Z Hotel's offer and work there at night.

I was working 16 hours a day in these kitchens and it began to wear me down. I had barbering skills and I loved cutting hair so I decided that on my time off, I would go to barber school. I attended Beauty School of America on 163rd and Biscayne Blvd on my two days off from the Ritz Carlton and my two nights off from Z Hotel. I had a full load; every hour and every minute of the day was accounted for. After finishing barber school and getting my license, I got a job at the Barber Lounge.

While in school, I had taken some lessons and tips from the famous, Ivan Zoot, who was known for his speed and precision and which was on record in the Guinness Book of World Records. People really never knew that my first passion was cutting hair. I already knew how to cut course hair but I wanted to diversify my skill set and learn to cut fine hair. They used to call me the prejudiced barber because when someone black would enter the shop, I would spin my chair opposite of their direction because I wanted to learn how to cut different ethnic hair so that I could work in any salon. I wanted to travel and work throughout the world and I wanted my hand in barbering to be just as diverse as my hand had become in cooking.

When I worked on South Beach at the Barber Lounge it was phenomenal. It was like a club and a barber shop all at the same time, girls would be dancing in bikinis while people were getting haircuts, you could order a drink, there was a hookah lounge, and big screen TVs, a DJ booth, and we all made money. We had to take turns going out on South Beach soliciting customers and they would love when I would go out because I was a talker and I would return with a train of people following me that would fill up the entire shop.

Most of my clientele were hotel and restaurant staff because we all stuck together to support each other and they had become my family. They would bring their kids and tell their friends. I was a chef by day and a barber in the evening and at night. It was easy for me to pass my barber exam because some of the test theory was based on bacteria which I had learned from the books that I had picked up in the prison library. There is nothing more seductive to a woman than a man who can cook and style hair. I would go to salon interviews in my chef jacket and they would be thrown off and tell me that they thought that I was in the wrong place and then I would whip off my chef jacket to reveal a barber's jacket underneath and they would go crazy! I was dual traded and it always made good conversation in the barber shop.

Fine cuisine is not in my cultural background and it took discipline to learn to be able to create the taste, the texture, and the look of the dishes served at these restaurants I was working at. There were some executive chefs who had come from high pedigree prestigious culinary schools, but my skills and passion and determination could not be denied.

At the Z Hotel, I was cooking for and meeting celebrities like Jada and Will Smith…and then there was Lebron James' coach…and then there was Precious. I couldn't believe that I was cooking for these people.

Eventually I was doing my own dishes and running specials. Following the Thanksgiving dinner service, I had made a deboned stuffed turkey with an avocado mousse and plantain chips and a seafood ceviche. A journalist came into the restaurant by coincidence that night and was so impressed by the meal they asked the restaurant management if the chef who prepared it could appear on the local news for a special feature on how to use Thanksgiving leftovers.

Although I was the one who had prepared the food, the executive chef tried to steal the limelight and showed up at the station to take this opportunity to try to promote himself instead. I invited my sister to share this experience with me and she was almost more excited than me, but when she saw that the executive chef was trying to take the spotlight for my work, she became outraged.

I felt like I couldn't say much because I was a felon and I was just glad to be working and seeing my food going on TV. But the journalist who had eaten my food and invited me to do the feature sensed what the executive chef was trying to do and not only voiced her opposition to my being sidelined, but in the moment, pushed me on stage in front of the camera.

Once I started talking, I created a presence that was magnetic and undeniable. After this feature, I was invited back to make solo appearances three times after that.

Even though I spent every waking hour working, I was paying rent and bringing home food from the restaurant every night. My sister's friends, the owners of the house, seemed to be okay with me staying there for a little until I could get my own place. I was also giving my sister money to help her take care of my niece and nephew, but she would come back daily demanding more, sometimes showing up at my job. When I finally refused to give her more, she put me out of where we were staying. Technically, she didn't have the authority to do so and I was encouraged to stay by the owner, but I wanted to avoid conflict.

I took my things and the money that I did have and headed back to South Beach. I ended up living at the Ritz Carlton rent free. I moved into the employee locker room right under their nose. The employee lounge and locker room were so big that I was there for two weeks undetected until a guy in the same situation found me out. His name was Jamie, a white guy from New Jersey who came right up to me and asked me if I was clean. I said yes, and he told me he knew a place where I could stay: a sober living program, and if I was interested to meet him after work then he would take me to the location.

To my surprise, it was a group of very nice condos managed by Tom who was the group leader. He explained that the terms of the living conditions were that I had to take a urine test every week and attend meetings. I stayed in this program for three years while I attended barber school and started at the Art Institute of Fort Lauderdale for cooking.

Everything was working in my favor until the day my niece and nephew came to my job. It had been almost a year since I had left my sister and her family with her friends. One of the waitresses came in the kitchen and said, "Terrence, you have visitors. They asked for Uncle Terry!" I knew exactly who it was. I came out front and there was my nephew and niece.

"How did y'all get here and how did y'all find me?" I questioned.

"Facebook!" my nephew exclaimed excitedly. "I seen you in a picture in front of this place. I knew how to find you in seconds." They had told me everything that happened to them within the last year. My nephew insisted that I get him and his sister a bus ticket to go home to Alabama. I was concerned about my sister's well-being, so I went against my best thinking and followed them to their new home. I was putting my sobriety at risk. I had heard about the neighborhood Brownsville a.k.a. Brown Sub. My sister got a new place there in the ghetto. And it was not a good location. Too much fighting, no food, and my sister couldn't hustle the system like she normally could. Right down the street was the Pork & Beans projects (Liberty Square), so named for the food the residents ate.

I walked in the door with Morgan and Kory. My sister looked surprised. "I don't want to fight with you, we need your help," was the first thing that came out her mouth. Her husband was sitting in the middle of the floor crying like a baby. Florida had kicked their ass from South Beach to Biscayne Boulevard and I was next.

You see, people see the pretty side of Miami on TV and then think all of Florida is the same. But Miami is like Detroit with palm trees. I've never seen so many homeless people in my life. Miami is drug infested. I let the drugs take me over again. It was the beginning of my relapse, a downward spiral that made me lose both of my jobs due to no call, no shows, and eventually losing my place due to dirty urine. I got my last paycheck and got on the bus to West Palm Beach, battered, beaten, and bruised and almost had a mental breakdown.

Getting any job is tough and cooking comes with its own set of challenges, but those were only intensified by my criminal record. Some people accept your skills, and some don't, especially with that F on my report card – here, F stands for *Felony*. If I could get through the basic application process with that F, getting a job in a kitchen usually included a test on paper first and then a practical culinary test or cooking stage, and with a face-to-face opportunity, I knew I had a chance at getting the job.

When I interviewed at Eau Hotel in Palm Beach, Florida, I studied their menu and tested very high on the cooking exam. There were three other people interviewing for the job. The interviewer came out in the lobby and she stopped at each candidate to greet us. As she got to me and she looked down at the paperwork and back up at me and asked, "Terrance L. Wallace?" I said yes and stood up. She said, "Terrance, can you wait a minute?"

The head chef came out and asked where I received my training and I told him that I had a lot of hands-on training and had participated in a correctional culinary program, which was why I learned a lot more material. His lips turned up at the corners but somehow, he didn't sound pleased when he said that so far, I had beaten out his prime candidate for the position. The next part of the interview consisted of the culinary test where we were given a series of items to cook and prepare. I overheard the head chef telling the other candidates that, "Everybody has bad testing days, but you can beat him out with your cooking skills - as a convict, there's no way that he can beat your experience in cooking." When they let us in that kitchen and turned on the stoves, I moved with speed, precision, and confidence, and I crushed it - their asses were mine.

I got the job, but that chef taught me every day. Even if I was on-point, he always had some remark to make about my time in prison. I would double and triple check my work, but he always found something wrong.

The rest of the staff used to ask me why I allowed him to do that and just put up with it, but a person in my position has to get in where he can. Just to be average, I had to put my head down and take it and still be twice as good as the rest, but the day came that he pushed me too far. During the dinner rush, I was triple checking myself and I knew I was sending flawless dishes out to the diners. Still, he called out, "Repair!" as he pushed a dish back to me to be fixed, effectively stopping the rest of the food from going out to the table over nothing and backing up the rest of the orders that were still steadily coming in.

I thought to myself that he better watch his own ass, because I was coming for it. Today, there would be a funeral in the kitchen and the dishwashers would be the pallbearers to carry his ass out of the kitchen. I started applying pressure and I pushed so hard he couldn't keep up.

He was lost – in the kitchen we call it *being in the weeds*, and with the heat from the stovetop warming my face I asked him smoothly if he needed a weed whacker, making everyone down the line bubble over in laughter. The rest of the cooks were responding to me until he was no longer a factor and I dominated the line.

The repercussions of showing off my skills were almost instantaneous, having me going out the back door in handcuffs the very next day. The rest of the staff were buzzing with the way I ran the kitchen, there was a rumor that the management team wanted to speak to me and my co-workers were tossing around gaudy exclamations like, *you can take his job, no problem.* Jean, my friend in the kitchen, pulled me to the side and said, "Tee, watch your back, man. That guy be coming for you. You are a threat to his existence."

Fueled by the praise from my co-workers, I began to start pushing harder than I did before. I wanted his job, so I was going to run his ass out of the kitchen. The chef knew he couldn't out-cook me on skill alone and he used the only card he had to make me lose my cool: degrade me with his jail house jokes. His words ringing in my ears were like putting fuel next to an open fire and my food was going up in the window as though I were in possession of the recipe for success.

I was winning this battle until he touched the soup. He announced that the soup was cold and needed to be reheated, but I knew he was just trying to slow me down so that he could catch up. Eyeing the bowl that was steaming gently under the glaring kitchen lights, I said steadily, "No, the soup is up to temperature."

With too much force, he pushed the soup back over the line and the hot soup splashed in my face. That was it. I dropped everything I was holding and pushed my way past everyone on the line and said, "You want to see what we do to punks like you in prison?" It was pure rage in my eyes. I hit him with some shots that sounded like firecrackers and slapped him from the front of the kitchen to the back door. The only guy in the kitchen that could get close enough to stop me was my friend Jean, but by then, the police had already been called and I was put in handcuffs and paraded out the back by two uniformed cops.

Handcuffed in the back of yet another police car, I realized I needed to learn more tolerance so that whatever the situation, I couldn't let no one push me in a corner or put myself in a position to tempt the devil in any way. Unexpectedly, the rest of the kitchen staff came to my aid and they managed to explain to the police the series of events that had occurred over the last two days.

The police opened the door and handed me my chef knives and told me I was free to go. I was surprised, touched that my co-workers had stood up for me. I was unemployed again, but I was free.

2013-2014: ATLANTA

had finally done well in Florida, I was working two jobs, and attending barber school. I had a full load. I filled up all my time so there wouldn't be any mistakes in my recovery. I learned that Florida was very seasonal, the snowbirds would come in the winter and Florida would be dead in the summer. Chefs from all over world come and go during season. I had a lot of invitations to move out west or go to New York, but my first choice was the Black Mecca of the United States – Atlanta, Georgia.

The thing that attracted me to Atlanta was the southern style cooking. I was French trained, but I wasn't from Paris. My family was from the south and you would think southern cooking would be second nature to me; I had seen no skill set in cooking southern food, but I would soon learn that you can fuse southern style cooking with any cuisine and get that southern flair. I had to be an all-around chef so when I landed in ATL, I made it my first business to enroll in culinary courses and I began to attend the Art Institute of Atlanta.

This wasn't as easy as I thought it would be. I had to disclose my criminal history to attend the school. This should have been the first sign that this was not going to go well, but I did it. It was embarrassing and humiliating to me. It felt like here I am in 2014, talking about what I did in 1999. My stepbrother had come to Atlanta with me to help me complete job applications and to assist me in getting settled, because the world had changed since I had been incarcerated and everybody wanted an application to be completed online. Standing in front of a computer was like me standing in front of a spaceship looking for the manual to start it up. I am dyslexic and learn differently. I am a hands-on learner, if you tell me and show me, I can do it. I would later learn in life that, in educational terms, I am a tactile and audiovisual learner. I had it all in my head, but I would be fighting myself just to get it out. Sometimes it would make me frustrated, but I learned to seek assistance.

When Willie Jr. was helping me fill out the applications and when we would get to the criminal background part and he would look over at me and notice that I was getting a little tense. I would tell him to just ignore that part and leave it blank, but Willie Jr, being an honest guy told me, "No matter how you feel about it, put it on paper, just put it out there. There are only two things they can say to you, 'yes' or 'no'." He helped me to realize that I had been so ashamed of what I had done, but now I was free and this was my moment of truth. I wasn't going to hide anything from anyone, anymore. My substance abuse, my criminal record, I was no longer going to give anyone ammunition to use against me. I decided to put it out there first.

I accepted that the worst thing that I could hear was "No" and again there was what Chef Hill said in my ear all the way from Lakeland Correctional Facility, "You're going to hear a lot of 'no's'! But when you hear, 'yes', take full advantage of the situation." Chef Hill would always be brutally honest with us in class; he was preparing us for what was to come. He knew how we would be frowned upon in the food industry with a criminal record. He always used to say, "You can't work in a fine dining establishment with a half ass work ethic with a criminal jacket, you have to be twice as good, just to be looked upon as average."

I hit all the high-end hotels and went to interview after interview, but I got the same response from each regarding my criminal background: "I'll have to see if I can push this though Human Resources." When they first came out to interview me, they were giving off vibes of how dare you come in here to apply? But as I began to talk, they realized I had the skill set because I could speak the language of high-end cuisine fluently. I was bold enough to walk through that door and I would dissect and breakdown their whole menu, station after station, and I hadn't even walked into their kitchen.

After a month of interviews there was still no actual job offers for the positions that I applied for; I had applied for Executive Sous Chef or Sous Chef but there were only offers for much lower positions such as Lead Line Chef. You see, Atlanta is like this, everyone had the same idea to come to the Black Mecca seeking fame and fortune so the companies had the advantage, they could pay the minimum for first class workers. If you had a bachelor's degree, you better get a master's degree, if you could sing, you better learn how to dance at the same time, if you could act you better learn how to be a stunt car driver too, and if you were a preacher, you better know how to lead the choir and play the tambourine, guitar, and organ too. Atlanta wanted a full show, they wanted their bang for their buck. Atlanta had the ideology of 'same nigga, different face'.

My savings were getting depleted, so I had to take anything just to pay my bills and stay afloat. I was being lowballed in Atlanta and at the point of lowering my standards. I was used to making 20+ dollars an hour and I had to settle for $15 an hour.

The Hyatt hotel is where I got my first job and there, I would meet my longtime friend and mentor, Chef Paul O'Shea. He was a Patrick Swayze looking cool white guy from Ireland. I explained to Chef Paul O'Shea my whole life story and before the interview was over, I told him all I wanted was an opportunity. I told him if you let me in the back of the kitchen, I'll out cook every last chef that was in the back of the house. It was kind of bold and arrogant, but I wasn't going to be denied that day. He kind of laughed, but when he saw that I was dead serious, he took me up on the challenge. This is called a working interview. I crushed them all within an hour and the job was mine. I was back! This position was called Chef de Partie and I was promised that if I kept this pace up for six months, I would get the open Executive Sous Chef position. Chef

Paul and I became very good friends, he would tell me about his international travels, how he cooked for a Saudi Arabian prince, how he traveled around the world cooking for celebrities, how he traveled from hotel to hotel fixing their problems and once the hotel was running efficiently, he would move on to another hotel. It was a great job for a single man.

I had a different flair than other chefs in Atlanta. I'm not saying I'm the best chef, but I will say I'm a great student and what I've done is taken lessons from every chef I worked for and built an arsenal of recipes from different restaurants. Chef Paul could lay out a king's spreads and it was Chef Paul who gave me the room to create. I laid out spreads that looked like they belonged in a movie scene in a king's palace; the spreads were called *A Farm's Table* with all fresh food items, two fish items, two fresh soups per day, three fresh pasta items, fresh breads, fresh cheeses, and two fresh meat sandwich spreads. It was a sight to see, three kinds of fresh greens and fresh desserts and pastries. The hotel's percent of sales went from 33 percent to almost 100 percent every day and the servers all wanted to transfer to the day shifts because the tips were better when I was in the kitchen.

I had always worked in the back of the house and I had never mingled with the customers, but Chef Paul taught me how to interact with customers. I spent about an hour and a half a day on the dining room floor. Atlanta was a very health-conscious city and we had to be very knowledgeable of what we were serving. Our guests had special diets, some were vegan and some were just getting older and wiser and wanted to be aware of what they were putting in their bodies. I spent time asking them their likes and dislikes and I would greet everyone in the restaurant.

I had stolen the show, but I needed a change in my environment as it was putting my recovery in jeopardy. The women and the partying were both at my job – I didn't even need to leave work to party. I started bringing a change of clothing to work so I could slip right into party mode, but I started getting distracted from my goals and I would be so tired, I would fall asleep and would miss my stops on the train. I began to analyze my situation by using the tools that I had learned at SHAR House: recognizing when you are in the danger zone and how to ask for help. I was working so much that my armor wasn't safe anymore. I was so busy that I stopped attending my NA and AA meetings, but I would learn that this had to be a part of my daily routine like eating and using the restroom.

While I was in there, I worked and cooked for multiple celebrities such as Mike Epps, Angie Stone, Cassandra Davis, Evander Holyfield, Mama Dee, Waka Flocka and his wife Tammy, Sung Kang from The Fast and Furious, Khandi Alexander from NCIS, Ice Cube, Bun B from West Side Connection, Bishop Eddie Long, and Michael K. Williams.

My favorite celebrity was Mike Epps, who is so down-to-earth; he called down for room service all the time asking for my fried chicken. I made dishes for him that weren't on the menu and on my days off, Chef Paul would call me and say, "Hey your buddy is looking for you," and he would ask that I come in to prepare his meal. Even him and his manager, Bobby, came down to the kitchen and asked me if I would mind doing some outside catering. I explained to him that I wanted to start my own catering business, and he took pictures with me and told me I could use him as an endorsement to attract other celebrities.

Now Miss Cassi Davis from the House of Payne was full of fun, she would talk shit to you and then run behind her bodyguard who was so big he could block out the sun. It was always a pleasure to see her coming.

I ended up taking on another job at the City Club of Buckhead in Atlanta. Chef Darryl Evans, the former head chef at the City Club had just passed away. The Club was grieving his loss, but with the passing of Chef Evans, there would be an awakening of a new generation of chefs. Chef Evans was a trail blazer in the culinary world. He had been awarded the American Culinary Chef of the Year three times and had been the first African American member of the US Culinary Olympic team, where he won two individual gold medals and a team gold and silver medals; he was in the Chef's Hall of Fame; participated in the International Culinary Olympics; and had been on the World Cooks Tour for Hunger.

The Edna Lewis Foundation hosted a gala every year which was a grand affair, a coveted and honored event where both established and up-coming chefs gathered to showcase their talents to raise money for scholarships for culinary arts students. The foundation was established to celebrate the life and legacy of its namesake: a chef, cookbook author, and a teacher, who had defined and refined the American view of southern cooking. With the passing of Chef Darryl Evans, that year's gala also honored his work and his life. Chef Evans was no longer with us, but he left a legacy that was alive and thriving.

I was asked to participate in the gala's tribute dinner celebrating his life and I jumped at the opportunity to participate. To say that I was honored is an understatement and out of all the invitations that I have received in my lifetime, this experience is and always will remain a grand moment for me. I had worked my way from the prison yard to being in the midst of chefs from the Food Network and all regions of the world. The group of chefs that were asked to participate in this event were world class chefs. I was honored to be invited to such a prestigious event and I felt that I would be a part of something that would be remembered for years to come.

That morning my son and I left our Marietta home and jumped on public transportation to head out to the school in Tucker. You know, some people don't have faith in your dream and it broke and still breaks my heart that my son wouldn't accept the *new* me who was catching the bus to cooking events with him. He wouldn't even sit with me; he was ashamed of me because I wouldn't return back to hustling. Turning back to the streets was no longer a temptation in my life and I wanted nothing to do it. I had changed my whole mind set; I no longer even listened to or watched anything that was street related, period. I remember him saying once, "I would have stayed with mom if I knew I would be catching the bus with you all over town." I had been out of his life for five years when he was younger and since I had been back in his life raising him, I was making a diligent effort to break the pattern. I didn't want him to end up in the street; I was trying to steer him in a different way.

There were kids his age participating in this event and I overheard him talking with them, but there were two different conversations going on. He was talking about rapping and they were talking about cooking, but I was hoping that they would gain his interest. You do all you can for your kids, but sometimes their destiny is their destiny, no matter how hard you try. I wish I could tell you that my son joined me and accepted the knowledge that I had to pass along and that I managed to save my son from his destructive path, but that would be a lie. He's now serving time for murder and realizing that you can kill 100 people in one rap song, but if you kill one person in real life, you're facing life in prison. The street dreams that he had dug deep in his soul. Drug Dealer 101 was all he was interested in. He didn't want the new me, he wanted what he was told about me in the streets. I think he was trying to avenge my failures in the street and say that he was the new, improved Terrence Wallace.

The atmosphere at the event was electrifying. If you were in the building, it was like you made the NBA draft, but for the culinary arts world. The chefs gathered in the kitchen were all working together to make sure the guest had a 5-star experience – an experience of precision and detail where all of the plates looked the same, tasted the same, and were served perfectly in sync, all the plates hitting the table at the same time. The guests in the dining area were Chef Evan's wife and children, extended family and close friends, and all types of people who he connected with over the span of his career…famous chefs, dignitaries, celebrities, instructors, people from all over the world. There were about three hundred people and it was a black-tie affair, with everyone clothed in tuxedos and evening gowns. Those gathered were the chosen elite who were there by invitation only.

With the Edna Lewis Foundation Celebration Dinner on my resume, I had proof that I was a part of such a prestigious event and I figured now I had a platform to stand on to pursue other chef opportunities that would open doors for me. I started applying for top-notch chef positions all over Atlanta and it worked. I was offered a job at Renaissance Learning Center where I was in charge of providing food and a cooking class for kids. It felt great to be giving back to my community and I was happy with my achievements.

The Renaissance Learning Center was led by a passionate educator, Marie Johnson, who was the director and founder. The center had a spirit of youthful energy and being there felt like I was connecting with and giving back to the community and to see these little people show up in their little uniforms so eager to learn about cooking was a reward that was far beyond any amount of money. It was a blessing to me to be able to teach these children food nutrition and how to prepare meals and I don't know who was more excited, them or me. Even the parents and the teachers were excited.

Soon after I got there, Ms. Johnson confided in me that her food cost was tearing into her budget. After thinking about what she shared with me, I came up with an idea that could possibly help her. Since the center was a nonprofit agency and serving children who were from families with lower incomes, I was sure that there were some local, state, or government food programs that would alleviate her food cost. After a little research, making a connection, presenting the center's 501C paperwork, and completing an application, the problem was solved. We took the center's bus to the distribution site and we drove away with that bus loaded from the back to the front with hardly enough room for us to fit in there. I showed her management skills that I had learned in prison: how to do portion control, food cost, create labor budgets, and cost control. Ms. Johnson was so grateful. She was doing something great in the community and she didn't want to see her program be in jeopardy of failing or struggling due to food cost, so anything that I could do to help support her mission, I was on board.

I got a second job working nights at the W Hotel as an Executive Sous Chef. The W Hotel is located in the hustle and bustle of downtown Atlanta's central business district. The area was alive and vibrant, and it was close to the Georgia Aquarium, Centennial Olympic Park, and Coca Cola headquarters. The W Hotel had an air of sophistication. It's exterior and interior design was carefully and artistically designed. Everything about the hotel was modern, but it was a tasteful grand, not an over-the-top tacky grand. Everything had a place and everything was perfect. The hotel guests who stayed there were paying for nothing less than a perfect experience and it had to be perfection every single time. Prior to getting hired at the W Hotel's BLT Steakhouse, I had three cooking interviews in which I was observed and the dishes that I prepared were evaluated for taste, texture, and plating. Again, with this win, I felt that I had arrived.

I was happy with where I was in life. Working at the W Hotel satisfied my passion for indulging in the art of preparing fine cuisine. Working at the center was my feel-good experience of giving back to the community. But as soon as I was getting into my stride and feeling like I was on solid foundation, my past would catch up to me and become a waking nightmare. I was always totally honest about my past and my criminal record. I had done my time, but sometimes the future won't forgive your past and it impacts your present. I didn't see it coming, but I would have a series of events that would affect me in such a painful way that I would stop cooking for an entire year.

I came into work like any normal day, but as soon as I got there, I could tell something was wrong. Everybody was looking nervous and I was told the director of the program was looking for me. Ms. Johnson called me into her office and she asked, "Terrance, I know you have been honest about your past, but is there anything else you want tell me?"

"No ma'am," I replied. "I think I put everything down on my application."

"Damn," she sighed, disappointed. "I got a letter from the state of Georgia that said that you cannot be permitted to be on the property and if you're found on the property, my license will be taken."

"I'm not a child molester – I haven't hurt anybody, I just stole some money!" I protested. The letter she showed me was signed by the Director of the Georgia Department of Early Care and Learning and it stated that my file was incomplete, my status was undetermined, and that I could not be in the learning center while children were present. If I was found on the premises, her license to operate could be revoked. I had provided all the information on the application, so I didn't understand the language of my file being *incomplete* and *undetermined*. But when it came down to it, it was me or her business.

I left gracefully and with understanding towards her and I promised her that if she needed, to call me with any questions about continuing to get food through programs or any budgeting and planning for food, she was more than welcomed to call me. I left Renaissance Learning Center with a broken heart.

Less than a week after that, another bombshell hit home. The manager of the W called me into their office and expressed that something had come up about my background. What Willie Jr. had said about putting it out there was ringing through my head, but I had followed his advice and I had been honest. Georgia is a right-to-work, non-union state and because Georgia is a right-to-work state what this means is that in Georgia, employers have the right to fire you at any given time with no reason and with that, I was walked out of the back door.

Bad things come in threes and just after losing my jobs for reasons beyond my control, I was devastated again before I could even get a chance to regroup and put the puzzle back together. It started when I heard keys scraping against the lock of the condo I had purchased. Then there was a knock on my front door. I got up and opened the door to a little old white lady. "Can I help you?" I asked.

She stood back and double checked the house number. "You're in my house," she told me, trying to peer past me to look inside. At first, I thought she had Alzheimer's, like her caretaker had let her wander out of the house. I invited her inside and went upstairs to retrieve all my paperwork from the finance company to show her that I was the owner. Little did I know, all the paperwork that I had was worth nothing.

I had come to Atlanta seeking a fresh start, a second chance, and when I had arrived, the first realtor newspaper that I picked up was called *Second Chance Realtor*. I took this as a sign from God because I was walking in faith and Second Chance Realtors had such a good ring to it. The real estate agent was Sam Leccima, who had been featured on the second season of *Flip This House Atlanta*. He worked together with his wife and seemed like a black person that was trying to help black people rebuild their lives, so I reached out to them. Prior to the sale, I only saw his wife together with him and she wouldn't say a word, which I found somewhat odd, but I figured that she was just quiet and reserved. After I purchased a condo from them, some woman would call me from the corporate office to follow up and make sure that I was satisfied with my purchase; Leccima would show up in person each month to collect my payments, which at the time, I thought was his personalized approach to his Second Chance home buying program.

The little old white lady and I went to the condo management office. She had her paperwork and I had mine. They barely had to glance at my paperwork to tell me that it was worthless and that they had no clue who I was and that I definitely shouldn't be on the property.

Leccima and his wife had spun a web of lies and after making a home and being there for almost a year and a half, I was given thirty days to leave the premises.

Sam Leccima had been the property manager for the condo complex, so he had inside information. He knew when the residents would be away for extended periods working abroad and he knew which apartments would be empty. He and his wife seized this opportunity to set up fake sales of their property. He used his position as office manager for a front. They were truly a tag team couple. It was a scam and I had been cheated out of my money and made out to be an asshole by this con artist and his significant other.

He had taken my down payment and disappeared. I was court ordered to leave the premises. Not only had they toyed with me, but they had used my name, my image, and my story to sell their scam. When we got to court, one of the fellow complainants had a flyer with my image on it. She was outraged and insisted that I was a part of the scam. Her accusations incited an angry mob and now everyone's attention was on me. The police clutched his gun and for an hour, I was stuttering, trying to convince them that I had been a sucker too.

Leccima's wife was questioned and she begged the judge for leniency in his sentencing because they had three daughters. For the first time I heard her voice – it was the woman from the corporate office who had called to 'check in' on me. Now I had a face to the voice. I yelled out in a fit of rage, "She called me over the phone, that's the lady from corporate. She was in on it too!" They were the best that I have ever seen do it. I considered myself pretty much a player of the game as well, but the slick had gotten slicked – they sold water to a well.

2015: ALABAMA

Atlanta had stripped me of my pride, broke me down, and left me homeless. My son was still living with me and we packed our things and headed back to Birmingham, Alabama. Junior wanted so desperately to be around my family. My family moved away from Michigan when he was very young, so the only memories he had of his aunts and cousins were good because he was a kid, but he didn't know them as adults.

He would learn very quickly that they would charge you for breathing next to them. I let him stay with my mom and I went to stay on the other side of town with my brother Willie Jr.

I knew what the outcome would be, but I had to let him learn for himself and he did *real* quick. His stay with Shug would end when she used some abusive language and made some derogatory comments to him.

He began to get caught up in the atmosphere that they created and functioned within. Negative things were said about me which caused a rift between us, so I stepped away. I had always known how to generate money, so with my son at my Mom's house, they saw it as leverage for them to get money from me. My son was now stepping into adulthood, so I was no longer responsible for providing everything for him. When I wouldn't meet the requests and demands for money, the expectation was that my son would pay what was required to be present whether it was reasonable or not.

Junior wasn't used to having to pay just to be present, just to breathe. When things didn't go as planned and he began to see that he wasn't there out of loving kindness, he fell into a depression. He showed up in the middle of the night where I was staying and I was shocked and puzzled because I wondered how he got there and why he hadn't told me that he was on the way. He took a deep breath, looked at me and was like, "Dad, Grandma said some harsh things to me for no reason." He dropped his head and walked in. All I could say was, I told you so. I didn't know this that night and he didn't tell me, but he had bought a car. He didn't have a driver's license and had never driven on the highway, but that encounter with her had pushed him to drive himself in the middle of the night.

Shortly after I arrived in Alabama, I had gotten a job in a local barber shop, which was owned by a long-time barber in the community, Mr. Theo Eldridge, a very mild-mannered barber of more than fifty years. He had a *help wanted* sign in his door and I walked in, showed my Florida barber's certification, did a demo cut for him and just like that, I was the new barber at the shop. My family was under the impression that when they sat in my chair, haircuts were for free and wanted to benefit from my hair cutting skills just like they'd taken advantage of the fact I worked in restaurants. I had to pay booth rent when somebody sat in that chair, whether they paid or not, and eventually, my only way out was to ban all family members from my chair.

Cooking had broken my heart and I was pissed off at the whole system. This system that said that because I had a "F" on my back, I wasn't worthy of a chance to do what I loved to do. I had exhibited nothing but an exceptional work ethic, provided exceptional service and felt that I always brought that special something, that special touch that I had learned through years of working in fine dining. My love for cooking would not just go away that easy though. When I was working at the barber shop, people would just strike up conversations about food and I would go all the way in. I would have the whole barbershop in silence listening to me. I could prepare recipes from start to finish, giving full and vivid details on how the meal should be cooked at each step. The entire barber shop would become engaged.

One day when I was in the shop, a gentleman came in wearing chef pants and I greeted him and said, "Hey chef, do you need a haircut?". He seemed pleased that I recognized and referred to him as chef. As I cut his hair, we began to have a conversation and he told me where he worked, how long he had been cooking, and I shared with him that I was a chef as well. Before he left my chair, he had shared his concerns about new menu items at his restaurant and when he left the shop that day, he left with three new recipes. When he came back, he told me that the new menu items were great and he kept coming back for haircuts. Eventually, the word spread that there was a barber-chef who was cutting hair but who also really knew his stuff when it came to cooking. Soon after that, I had a large group of clients from the restaurant industry who were coming to me not only for haircuts, but to talk restaurant talk and recipes, swap tips, and to talk about the tricks of the trade.

In the meantime, I would sometimes bring in food to the barbershop for everyone to taste and some days, during lunch, I was preparing entire meals for all of us with a hotplate and a microwave. Even some of the customers got in on the action and tasted my cooking. The owner and the barbers would joke and say that soon we were going to have to start selling plates.

Mr. Theo would just listen to me and then one day he said to me, "You are a real chef, what are you doing in this barbershop?" I explained to him my background and what had happened in Atlanta. I explained that I was denied jobs because I was a felon. He said that I was blessed to have two skilled trades. He could see that cooking was my first love and cutting hair was just another gift that God had blessed me with. He convinced me to give cooking one more shot. He gave me a brand-new Bible the day I resigned from the barber shop and I still have that Bible to this day.

Before I left Alabama, my sister came to pick me up and take me to the nursing home. I watched my grandma (my mom's mom) take her last breath. I avoided my family as much as possible; there was a rumor flying around about what happened in Atlanta, but they had gotten the story all wrong, they weren't interested in the truth because gossip and lies sounded better to them. I didn't even try to defend myself. With this grandma's passing away and my other grandparents (who raised me) also dead, I was truly by myself. I looked around the room and realized the only person that truly gave a damn about me had just passed.

I had already decided that I would not attend my grandmother's funeral. I had attended my grandfather's funeral and when I viewed his body and kissed him goodbye there was a coldness that when through my body. It was a coldness that I felt for a long time after that day and all that I could see after that was him in the casket. I had disturbing dreams after that day and my spirit was not at rest. I wanted to remember my grandmother warm and as she was. I did not want to remember her in a casket.

I said goodbye to my grandmother the day she passed in the hospital. I felt that I was amongst people who did not genuinely care for me and I told myself that this was my chance to get a two for one. I didn't attend my grandma's funeral but I had one big funeral for every last one of them on the spot. From this day, I had no reason to look back at Alabama.

After my grandmother's death, I made the decision to seek out a sober living program, even though I was ashamed that I had failed in my sobriety, I knew that it would be stupid not to return and seek help. I was back to square one but I was also happy that I was getting my mind, body, and soul back together. I had great success in Florida and I felt that sun, the water, and the sand would be good for my healing.

I was told that the program had run out of funding and I was advised to seek more options in northern Florida which was the richest community in the United States. I started calling sober living communities in that area. I wasn't worried about transportation because Florida has an awesome public transportation system. I finally made the connection that would save my life. I was all set to leave; I made contact with a guy by the name of Peter Dacchille and I was the one with a countdown. I just had to hold on for about two weeks and during this wait, he called me every day to check on me. At first, I didn't think his concern was all genuine, I thought that he was after the money for the cost of the program, but later I would learn different. This guy would be the guide to answers about my addiction. This guy, out of everyone I meet in my life, would have the key to my success and I wouldn't fall short ever again. I would continue to grow from that point forward.

Before I left, I went to gather my things that I had left stored in my sister's garage. All of my furniture and worldly items were supposed to be stored safely and securely there since I hadn't had a place of my own to put them when I came back to Alabama. But as I walked in her house it was like déjà vu. I felt like I was walking in my own living room in Atlanta. My other family members had warned me not to leave my things at her house, but I didn't have any other options. She saw that I was upset but before I could say a word to voice my frustration, she began to recite the law to me about abandonment of property and that leaving things at a person's house without payment meant that she was entitled to any and everything left on her property.

Before I could get my hands around her neck, she threatened to call 911. She didn't care about an ass whooping, she could take a licking and keep on ticking. As I looked back at my things for the last time and I saw cigarette burns and Kool-Aid stains on all my hard-earned possessions, I told her, "This is your last time fucking me over," and I left out the door and cut my losses.

2016: FLORIDA

Peter Dacchille was waiting for me at the greyhound bus station in Florida. I had a new life to find and I had set all bullshit aside. Making this program work was a matter of life or death for me. Pete's program was intense. He asked a series of questions about how I felt, when the last time I relapsed, who I was around, what was I thinking, anybody who upset me. It was questions that I had never been asked and answering them allowed me to make connections and understand myself better than I ever had before. People think that you go off and get high, like you just do this thing randomly out of nowhere, but there has to be something that set you off.

There were more good times in my life than bad times in those days, so I was very open to answering the series of questions. When Pete was asking these questions, you could tell that he had been there, in the streets and you can see his growth and that he was genuine. I was willing to do whatever it took to participate in this program and get myself better.

Eventually I figured out that it was certain members of my family that triggered my addictive behavior. My saddest day came during an NA meeting. After sharing a problem with the group, the feedback that I received from them was straight forward and hit dead center. They told me, "Tee, you have another relapse in you if you don't stop going back to your family for approval."

I came to the realization that not everyone in my family was working to resolve their issues as I was and staying in that toxic environment would keep pulling me back into it. I had to make a choice, one of the hardest decisions I ever made. I had to use all the tools that I learned and change my surroundings. I had to stop living in shame and allowing people to shame my past behaviors.

I had similar realizations in the past, but finally, this time it sunk in and I accepted that my family wasn't good for me and that I needed to break these patterns. When I was around them, old memories and feelings resurfaced and I was heading straight for another relapse. They would cheer me on when I was doing well and I had money, but I knew it wasn't real. They would throw my past in my face and from the next room I would hear them talking, saying how it wasn't going to last. They were so negative and I knew that being around certain people would set me off.

To this day, Pete and I remain in constant communication. We make it a priority to talk at least once a week. As he travels the world and as I travel the world, we take the time to pause and fellowship and talk about working together. He has a new base location for his work which is in the rolling country foothills of Tennessee, The Magnolia Recovery Ranch, a sanctuary for individuals who are sick and suffering from the wrath of addiction. He can be contacted at peter@magnoliaranchrecovery. com.

During our group sessions, I also came to understand that I didn't need to internalize the harassment and discrimination I had experienced about my time in prison in past jobs. I had considered all the prison jokes as some hazing or punishment…I was just happy to have the job. Pete explained to me that it was bullying and I didn't have to just take it. I had the skillset. I wasn't going back to the street. I was determined that I was going to be a chef no matter what it took.

Prior to arriving in Florida, I had finally received my back unemployment of $4,000. But the treatment service wasn't cheap. I had to pay rent, attend classes, I had to attend service…the money I had depleted quickly over a handful of weeks and I was ready to look for a job. Florida was a very felony-friendly place. I was able to work in Florida, at places like the Boca Raton Resort, one of the best in the world – they would have royalty come in, people that come in from yachts. I ended up getting another job at Office Depot headquarters, where I would work in the morning from 7am to 3pm, then I would go to the Boca from 4 to 11pm.

It was a growing process for me and I really enjoyed life between the program and work. All the guys who were in the program wanted to be and we were there for each other in any way we could. Until I saved up enough money to buy a car of my own, I had a friend named

Robert from the program that would drive to pick me up from any bus stop that I was at and drop me off at another job.

I had seen these beautiful mega yachts and I wanted to learn how to work on these ships. One day I saw an ad in the paper for a job on board one, and it was paying $25 an hour. In 2009, that was good money! I had never made that much money and I went and applied, and they took me out on a couple of trips around Star Island, where we would cook lunch and dinner for the owners. I worked Monday through Friday at Office Depot and the Boca, so I had weekends off to work on the yacht. I always kept myself busy.

On one such weekend, I was driving myself to work on the yacht and stopped at a red light. All of a sudden, the world was shaking and I felt my body being slung around the car, like my one side of my body went one place and the other side of my body went another. The only thing that held me in place was the seatbelt. I hit the steering wheel so hard that it made a gash inside my chest, it felt like my body was being pulled apart by this force that I had no idea what was going on. When it all stopped, I thought for a moment there had been an earthquake.

When I tried to move to get out of the car, I couldn't. I felt warm and wet and when I looked down, I realized I had urinated on myself. I looked behind me and the whole back seat was folded in like crumpled aluminum foil. The whole trunk of the car was in the back seat. People who had gathered around were telling me to be still so I didn't injure myself more. Someone was apologizing and babbling about being late for a doctor's appointment. I realized I had been rear-ended by an 80-year-old lady. She hit me so hard that she hurt me because she had lifted the whole car up from the back.

They took me to the hospital. My main worry was that I'm down here in Florida by myself. If I didn't have any money to pay for my treatment services, then Pete was going to put me out. I couldn't go back to Alabama. So, I told the hospital staff that I was okay. They kept me overnight for observations and the next morning I still couldn't move. I still attempted to go to work: I was a workaholic. Working was my device for staying sober. To stay clean, I surrounded myself with being busy like I still do today. If I stay busy, I can't get into any mischief.

But she exploded my L3, L4, and L5 discs in my back. The doctors told me that I would never walk right again if I didn't get this operation. I ended up getting this operation. They put some titanium screws in my back, but within a week after the operation, the titanium screws broke inside my spine due to some manufacturing issues from the company, Amedia a.k.a. Spinal Elements. When I went back to the doctor, Jeffrey Katzell, he eventually started giving me the runaround and quit talking to me. They both left me hanging. I found out that in Florida, a doctor could perform surgeries without having any medical malpractice insurance. He had the nerve to charge me for a failed surgery and ruined my credit. I was a half a million dollars in the hole with a broken back. Afterwards, I not only had broken screws, but I had three separate blood infections from the broken metal that entered my blood stream and with one wrong move, I could be potentially paralyzed.

The old lady who hit me had some insurance but it wasn't really much and couldn't cover what I needed. I didn't have money for another operation, I didn't have money to stay on the medication, and I was constantly in pain. I was forced to leave Florida. Out of the blue, Chef Paul O'Shea, my buddy from Atlanta called, telling me that he had a job for me working a yacht club in the Hamptons in New York. I didn't even know where that was. He told me New York and that he'd start me off at 70 grand. So, I didn't really tell him the severity of how hurt I was. For 70 grand, I was all in and I would crawl there if I had to.

When you think of New York, you think of 24-7 nonstop, the city that never sleeps. I was conditioning myself to learn how to catch the trains, I had some experience in Atlanta, but it was nothing like New York. I was told the location to report and it was called Montauk Yacht Club. It was in Long Island, New York. I didn't know the difference between New York City and Long Island. As I was driving, I was confused and I wondered where all of the buildings were, this was not the NYC that I had seen on Law and Order. It was serene and quiet and I drove through the woods for about an hour and a half from the airport and all of a sudden, it opened up and it was like driving into heaven. The ocean was shiny as glass and it is still the most beautiful scenery that I have ever seen and I have been around the world at least three times.

When I got to the Hamptons in New York, it was phenomenal. Chef Paul made me second-in-command and they housed me as well. There were people being flown in from all over the world to work for the season. We even had interns from Canada. Being second-in-command was new to me, I was involved in the executive decisions. I had respect from my peers. I was no longer Terry from the hood. I oversaw large catering events and wealthy clients who come there for privacy. There was no taking pictures or asking for autographs. This was strictly prohibited. All these big mega yachts were coming in and we were cooking for all these big celebrities. I saw Puff Daddy, Dr. Phil, I even met Robert De Niro. Donald Trump's first wife Ivana was one of the guests that was there. Rhianna, Kanye West just to name a few, were all summering in the Hamptons. Some were nice and some were not so nice though, I ain't the one to gossip and you ain't heard it from me.

Montauk Yacht Club was built by Carl Fisher, a friend of Al Capone and it became a haven for the rich and famous during Prohibition. One of the highlights of my experience at Montauk was working with executives from Wall Street and other big corporations on team building exercises. They had to step out of their board room and into my element, the kitchen, to learn how to work together. It was an experience to work with these fortune 500 company executives who were making million-dollar decisions, take instruction, and guidance from a former prisoner and drug addict. They were in my domain and they treated me with the utmost respect. When they left, they showered us with gratitude, praise, and gifts.

The next important role that I had was as mentor and supervisor of four teenager interns from Canada who wanted to become chefs. Chef Paul O'Shea quickly handed them over to me. I think they had watched too much TV and got caught up in the glamour and the glitz that Hollywood sprinkles on cooking shows. They were a bit wild and didn't realize the discipline that it takes to make it look like magic, but there was one that stood out among the rest. He stayed after hours, he worked hard, and he listened. He would be right behind me at every step that I took and hung on to every word that I said. I had to be careful with my words and actions because they were looking at me and trying to imitate me. At that time, I felt that I had failed my son. It was my duty to raise him and somehow, I felt as if I had made a misstep along the way and he had gone astray. But as I worked with these young men, I realized that it wasn't me. Every person has a chance and an opportunity every morning that we get up. What you do with that opportunity is on you. The intern's name is Joseph Heung and he became known as grasshopper. He still writes me to this day. In our last text, he told me that he was a police cadet in Canada and that he appreciated all that I taught him and that the people skills and the life lessons that he learned that summer have helped him along the way.

During that time in Montauk, Chef Hill contacted me and said that a reporter from the *Detroit Hour Magazine* would be calling me to interview me for an article in which he would be featured. I had been one of his top students and I was also going to be a part of the article. The article, *"Culinary Program at Michigan Prison Nourishes Raw Talent"* was written by Dorothy Hernandez and was published on December 2, 2016. Below is an excerpt from that article:

No Prejudice with Food

The food industry is known for being generous with second chances.

"Food doesn't have any prejudice," says Terrance Wallace, who participated in the food technology program when he was incarcerated from 2004-07. "If you put up a good plate and it tastes good, someone wants to know who made that" and they don't care what their race is. Or if they were a former prisoner.

Wallace never forgot the advice executive chef Hill gave him: "You're going to hear a lot of 'noes' but the 'yeses' you hear you better take full advantage."

After he got out of prison, Wallace enrolled in culinary school and worked his way up through the ranks, even when some employers were wary of putting him in chef positions because of his record.

Eventually the noes were replaced with yeses. Wallace was an executive sous-chef the Montauk Yacht Club in New York, and he recently accepted a job as executive chef of a resort in St. Thomas in the Virgin Islands.

2017: ST. THOMAS, USVI

was doing so good at the yacht club in the Hamptons that they promoted me and sent me to St Thomas in the U.S. Virgin Islands. Nobody had ever offered me an opportunity to travel and I was given $20,000 to relocate. I was told that I was going to be the executive chef of this waterfront property.

When I first flew in, what I saw was nothing that I could ever imagine. I saw houses built into the sides of hills and everything seemed like it was going upward for what seemed like miles and miles into the sky. I secured housing prior to arriving on the island and the agent told me that it was about four miles from my job; however, they forgot to tell me that most of the distance was up a road that was carved into a spiraling hillside. The thing that blew my mind was that they were driving on the opposite side of the street with left hand steering, and the roads were very narrow.

The drive up and down the mountainside was breathtaking, where I would see full green trees and fruit trees all along my journey: mangos, bananas, plantains, avocados just sitting there waiting to be picked. When you reached the bottom, you were in town and my journey took me along the beach where there was sparkling blue water and you could see clear to the sand. As I continued my ride, I would see colorful fruit stands with all types of different fruits and vegetables that I had never seen or worked with before. I would also see the fishermen, mostly referred to as the Frenchies, with their roadside stands selling the fish that were native to the island: Old Wife, Hind, Yellow Tail Snapper, Grunt, and Spider Lobster. What I didn't know at the time, which I would learn later and think was not so cool, was there were very few fishermen of African heritage and they would be the ones posted up in the bush close to their stands cleaning the fish. It would make me think "Why didn't they own boats and why weren't they also catching and selling fish?"

There were more boats than there were cars and some marinas had their own zip codes. There was even a small island that I would see that was constantly lit up at night. It was somewhat of a mystery to me and the local women seemed frightened by just the mention of this island. When I started to inquire more about this place, I was told that some women went over there and weren't seen or heard from again. I later found out that this island was called Little St. James Island and it was the home of Jeffrey Epstein, also referred to by some as the Island of Sin, Orgy Island, and Pedophile Island.

St. Thomas was lively at night. You had Red Hook, Crown Bay, Yacht Haven Grand, Havensight, Waterfront, and Country. The favorite beach of the locals is Coki Point where the marijuana smoke was so thick, you could cut it with a knife. Magen's Bay is a favorite for the tourist and is said to be one of the most beautiful beaches in the world.

Cruise ships would pull into Crown Bay and Havensight about three times a week and the town center of Charlotte Amalie would come alive for the next six hours. As a chef, in a new territory, you are not the leader of the pack, you become a student of the territory. I learned some new things to make: drinks such as sorrel, tamarind, ginger beer, passion fruit, peanut punch. The traditional morning meal of johnny cakes with tart sauces of guava, coconut, pineapple and bush tea. Pastries like peanut and coconut sugercake. And the famous pates (empanadas) of chicken, beef, and saltfish. Main dishes and soups included blood pudding, seafood kalaloo, pork kalaloo, goat water, bullfoot soup, pigtail souse, saltfish and rice, and ducana, saltfish, and spinach.

Once I got down there and started working, I was sailing throughout the Caribbean and meeting so many celebrities: Justin Bieber; Oprah Winfrey; John Travolta was flying his helicopter all around the island; the Apple people were coming down on their mega yacht. I really loved the islands; the people were really friendly. I was having a good time, life was grand. I was finally making peace.

I found out that the yacht club was notorious for bringing outside talent instead of hiring locals. They are hard-working people but their training was limited because they didn't have any culinary schools on island. The locals who worked at the yacht club told me they had been working on their jobs for five and six years with no raises, only making about $8 bucks per hour. When I brought it up to the general manager, he defended it by stating that they give them Christmas bonuses, so they should be happy with that. This guy and I weren't gonna see eye to eye, because I believe in treating people fairly. I never thought you could discriminate against your own race of people, but this guy was truly a "Mister Charlie," a term that was used in the African American community to refer to an imperious white man or in some instances a black man who is arrogant and perceived as acting white.

I used the skills I had picked up in the prison library and negotiated the back surgery claim myself. I ended up getting $208,000 to cover my surgery but I thought to myself, after I pay for this operation what am I going to do? I decided to take a risk with the money. I bought me a food truck and everything I needed to make it happen and I shipped the whole food truck to St Thomas.

I had some of the people that work at the restaurant come work for me in the food truck part-time, so I was doing really good. A lot of the customers from the yacht club would come over to my food truck. When the yacht club's general manager caught on to what was happening, he thought I was poaching their customers. "People are following you guys to the food truck," he stated, giving me an ultimatum. "You have to make a choice between us or the truck."

I thought what I do in my own time was my own time. He thought he was slick, but he wasn't slicker than me. My contract was to be with them for two years down there and so I took my cell phone to the next meeting to record everything he was saying. "So, you're telling me that I can't work my food truck on my time off?" I asked, trying to bait him. "If I work my truck on my own time, that I'm fired?"

He was so stupid that he nodded, and said sincerely, "Yes. That's exactly what I'm saying."

I just smirked at him and said, "Man, I'm gonna work my trailer."

He told me that I was fired, and so I took the recording and emailed it to corporate. Corporate settled out with me for the two years of my contract.

One of the girls that worked for me told me I should start selling Johnny Cakes and bush tea, a tea made from local lemongrass. I agreed to try it out and when I arrived at the food trailer the next day, there was a line of people that were waiting for me to open. I was so excited because I had never had a line waiting for me and I had a full fledged breakfast menu. As I arrived, I greeted the customers and told them to let me fire everything up and they were so patient and continued to wait. I started cooking bacon, potatoes, eggs, sausage, pancakes, and I started counting all of the heads and calculating the dollars that I would make off of breakfast.

As I opened the window and started taking orders, order after order, it was Johnny Cake and bush tea. After about fifteen orders, I yelled out of the window to the rest of the line in frustration, "Who is here for breakfast?" Johnny Cake and bush tea only sell for one dollar each, so out of fifteen customers, I only had $30 and I had cooked up a whole week's supply of groceries within one hour. When I realized that no one was there for my full fledged breakfast menu, I yelled, "No more Johnny Cakes or bush tea, go back where you've been going."

Out of spitefulness, a native woman walked up to my counter and snatched my whole stack of menus and held them hostage and yelled, "This is false advertisement." I pleaded with her to give the menus back because I had just spent $150 getting them printed. She drove around with them for two days and she taunted me, shaking the menus out of the window as she drove by. I had to make an agreement that I would sell Johnny Cakes just to get the menus back.

On another occasion, I had advertised that I was selling yellow tailed snapper and I also had a thing I called, *You Hook It, I'll Cook It.* People would bring me the fish that they would catch on charter trips and I would cook it and add the side items. Most of the time, it was a good deal and people would give me the extra fish, which I could sell for profit.

I almost made one costly mistake when I cut the head off of one of the customers fish and disposed of it. I had never heard of eating the heads of the fish. As I gave her the order, she was pleased and she said, "Smells good." Four minutes later, I saw her pull into the parking lot like a stunt car driver. She said, "You shortchanged me, Mister."

As I opened the box and saw that everything was intact, I asked, "What's wrong?"

She replied, "Where's my head?"

I said, "What head?"

She said, "You know what I'm talking about, Yankee boy…you trying to make fish soup with my head…I want my head or I want a discount."

I said, "You want me to get the head? I threw it away."

She insisted that I get it out of the trash and I did. I dug it out of the trash and washed it off and as I cooked it, I watched the fish watching me cook him. Lesson learned: learn the ways of the locals.

Before I left, I had a conversation with one of the guys who was one of my regular customers at the yacht club. I'd always bring him the food myself when I knew he was sitting in the restaurant. "Sorry if this is out of line," he started, "But how much money you make in a year?"

"About $80,000 a year," I told him honestly, wondering where he was going with this.

"That ain't shit!"

"What?" I asked, taking a breath so I didn't get irate with him or nothing. "What could I be doing different that I could make more money?"

"Your food looks like that, you should be on a super yacht!" he said enthusiastically, pointing at himself. "I make $160,000 in 9 months working on these yachts. Your food is incredible! The type of job you're doing, working at a land-based restaurant, this is for locals."

Yacht work was outsourced to people from different countries around the world; the locals were not working on the yachts as there was not any training. Young foreigners came down there to enjoy the tropics and party and make all their money and go home. Many Virgin Islanders really only made steady money during the tourist season, working in service industry positions in restaurants and hotels to make ends meet.

I hired three groups of locals to help me with my food truck and then I got about 25 resumes together and started pounding the yacht yard. The yacht docks private and usually gated off, but a good friend was in charge and he let me through. I went from ship to ship knocking on the door, introducing myself and they would take my resumes and say, "Sure, we got a chef right now, but all my friends, they're always looking for somebody!" It was an unbelievable job market. I ended up sailing around the islands, St. Thomas, St. John, St. Croix, Puerto Rico, the British Virgin Islands, St. Kitts, the Grenadines, all the way down to Trinidad. I was doing these runs every weekend and I was making money hand over foot.

I had built a life for myself; I was drug free, and all the demons from my past - I had put them to rest. I was an active member in the community, I was going to schools teaching kids how to cook, I was doing career day, anything that anybody asked me to do as far as charity work. A lot of the kids would come up to me after all excited and say, hey man I want to be a chef! I felt that I had a purpose now. Then the pain in my back started again and I knew that I would have no choice but to get another operation.

The screws had broken in my spine. It was an unbearable pain. I tried to contact the company several times, I called back and forth. I even tried to file a lawsuit, but it was such a big company that nobody would touch them. At this point in time, I was still half a million dollars in the hole with medical bills and they never tried to assist me with anything, didn't even pay for a single band-aid. Not only was my business down, I also ended up having bad credit because of an injury. I had to save up enough money to get my operation. I couldn't even get up and go to the food truck myself, but my employees were loyal. I had two Dominican girls who ran that food truck like they were trained drill sergeants. One of them would have to come get the keys to get to work and open up.

When the pain that I was experiencing became unbearable, the second operation became mandatory. I could not wait any longer and so I left the Virgin Islands and headed to Miami for the operation. The day after I flew out of the Virgin Islands to get my operation, Hurricane Irma, a category 5 storm, hit the islands. It took a long time for information to reach the mainland, because all phone towers and internet lines were down following the storm and days passed before I could get in contact with my people and make sure they had survived. Finally getting to see videos and pictures was devastating. It looked like a bomb had dropped on the island. All the luscious green trees were gone. Roofs were blown away, windows had exploded, houses sliding down the side of the hills. Paradise had turned into a fucking war zone. Hurricane Maria blew through the islands just ten days after Irma, another category 5 storm that wiped out anything that had survived the first.

In the Virgin Islands, I had a fresh new start; I was building a new life and a new home. All I wanted was to return to the islands and help the recovery process, but I needed to recover from a major surgery myself. After my surgery, I needed to wear a body brace – like a bionic iron man suit. The doctor told me I needed to wear it for two years minimum and then he said, "Man, you can't go back over there now, a hurricane is no place for you to recover." They had cut me from my booty crack all the way up to the middle of my back and I had 58 staples in my back. I would be trying to walk and bleed down the inside of my pants, but I just couldn't give up.

My doctor insisted that I couldn't go back to the island. Many people had left the island and the ones who didn't were there to deal with what happened as a result of the hurricanes - no electricity, a limited food and water supply, and some with damaged housing or no housing at all. Resources were limited including lack of medical professionals and medical care. My doctor made sure that I didn't attempt to go back to the islands by putting me on a no-fly list. I couldn't go back there at this moment and physically I needed to get better.

But I had no home in Florida. I only had my room for a week and a hotel room that I had gotten in West Palm Beach. I couldn't do anything for myself, not even sit on the toilet and wipe my own butt. I needed to ask for help. It was hard. I called my sisters to come and get me and I had to lay down in the backseat the whole way to Alabama. While they thought I was asleep, I overheard my sisters whispering to each other, "I hope he has some money left." I was literally helpless and they wanted to take what little I had left to maintain me. At my sister's house, I had to sleep wrapped in a paper bag because she had cockroaches so bad in her place that they would crawl up in my bandages.

I refused to take the medication they prescribed me for my pain because I had already beat that demon. I had an addictive nature and I'd be damned if I was going to dance with the Devil again. I just dealt with the pain: some days were easier and some days the pain would make me tremble and shake and bite my lip, and I would just grit down and lay still and hope the pain would pass. I had no quit inside of me, even when I ran out of insurance for physical therapy. I had never been in that position before and I did everything I could to get myself back together. I would go to the YMCA to float in their pool to learn how to walk again and I started doing volunteer services at the church, whatever I could to get on the best side of God. I felt that God didn't bring me that far in life to just to give up on me.

2018: VIRGINIA

I called my sister and went to stay with her for a while. I kept accumulating these pills because I refused to take the medication they prescribed for my pain and they just kept sending them to me by mail. There were boxes and boxes of them, I had a couple of thousands of these Percocet pills, some type of opiate. I thought my family members were concerned about my well-being, asking me questions about the operation and what medication I was on? Their eyes would light up when I'd explain and they would grab their necks saying, oh… I'm in so much pain, do you think I could get one of them?

One time I gave one to my cousin and after she popped it in her mouth I watched her transform, like she had just activated slow motion mode. "Do you know how much those are worth? $20 per pill!" she informed me afterwards, asking me how many I had. I knew my stash easily had over 2000 pills and that I couldn't do a thing if anybody tried to rob me or take my medication. I was in a full body bionic traction suit! But people started coming around and were trying to turn me back into a drug dealer. They would give me money for some of them and I didn't want that.

"I gotta leave here," I told my sister one day. "I can't let my circumstances change me for who I am. I'm a chef. I'm not going to get caught up in these streets again."

The next morning, I caught the train to Michigan by myself. I went north to Michigan to stay with my brother for a while and that didn't work either. I wasn't supposed to be moving around like that and they had to lift me up to get me on the train. I was glad to see my son and my stepdaughter. Even though Sky and I had split up almost fifteen years ago, I still loved and cared deeply for her daughter. She had just had a baby, so I met my first grandchild. My son was 19 by this time and making his own choices.

But getting to Michigan was like getting out of the pan and jumping straight into the fire. If I moved too strenuously, I would start bleeding because I still had those 58 staples holding my back together. I felt so helpless, I could barely walk. My best friend came over to take care of me. It worked for a little while, but my existence was just another money pit. Every time I looked up someone was knocking on the door needing money. Here I am laying on my back, able to do anything for myself at that time people still pulling that.

My friend Alicia, who lived in Virginia reached out to me and invited me to stay with her and recover. Before I went to the Virgin Islands, I had met her at a gas station in northern Virginia. She held the door for me and I commented that she had good manners. I invited her to follow me on Facebook and she did. At the time, I didn't know if we would see each other again or under what circumstances we would see each other. Throughout the years, we talked and became confidantes. We would talk on the phone and we would agree, disagree, agree to disagree, and at times just disagree to agree. Our conversations were simple and we were just getting to know each other. We were getting to know each other a little at a time. I was a free spirit and I moved when and where the opportunity took me. We talked about seeing each other, but opportunity for this never happened for whatever reason. I had told her that I wanted to share my story with the world and write this book and she encouraged me to start putting it on paper.

This was all right after my accident, and I was in pain when she met me, but I shielded my pain. As I said before, I was living with broken screws in my back. We would talk, and I would tell her about my travels and I would Facetime her and show her my world. She was a schoolteacher and what drew me to her was that she taught in a juvenile detention center. She probably could have taught anywhere, but this is what she chose to do and this caught my attention.

She was aware of some of the things that I was experiencing while staying with my siblings and she encouraged me to come to Virginia. She said that she lived alone and encouraged me to come there to heal, relax, and regroup and eventually I agreed. I expressed to her that I was in pretty bad physical shape because I wanted her to know exactly what was going on with me, but that didn't stop her from encouraging me to come.

The plan was that I would go there and begin to strategize and build myself up to return to the islands and in the process begin to write this book and get to know her a little more. She had offered to come and get me because she didn't want me to get on a train and make that long journey, but I didn't want her to have to drive to Michigan and once I made up my mind to leave and go to her in Virginia, I was ready to leave.

She picked me up at the train station. It was October and the night air had a little chill to it, but it was nowhere as cold as it had been in Michigan. We had talked a lot so it didn't feel like we were strangers, but there was a little nervousness at first because we would now be staying in the same space, and she had been used to living alone. Our favorite activity became going to the local library to check out DVDs, because she was a cheapskate and did not have cable. We watched every boxed set of Law and Order, even the British version. There was comfortable silence with her, and I could make phone calls, lay plans, and rest up.

I eventually began to get out a little. I was still walking with a wide stance and my walk was very unsteady. I didn't really trust my body. I was weak and in so much pain, but I was determined. I started taking short walks around the neighborhood. I found a church a few blocks away, and I started going to the services and helping them pass out baskets. I had a little shopping cart that I used to push around with me. I started praying again – *Lord, you know I don't deserve this. Please help me. Please help me, I need somebody in my life that is going to be there for me. Just to help me for me.*

Some time later, she had her grandson over one night. It was early morning and she was upstairs sleeping. I was in the kitchen when he came down. I asked him if he was hungry, and I began to whip out the pots and pans, taking out the food and explaining what I was going to cook. He got really excited and he made a request, "May I have cheese in my eggs please?" He would become one of my greatest little supporters.

After a few weeks of just cooking here and there, I began to think that I needed to start cooking again for real, and I told Alicia to invite her parents over for dinner the upcoming weekend. Before I could even begin to cook, I had to go out and buy a decent set of pots and pans. She had something that most people could put food in and cook, but I needed something that I, as a chef could work with, so we went to the Salvation Army to look for pots and pans. She seemed to doubt my ability to find what I needed in there, but lo and behold, I found an entire set of Cuisinart and some cast iron which would serve the purpose.

I was eager to get back into practice and the day that her parents came, I had turned the kitchen and dining room into a makeshift chef's kitchen. I cannot remember exactly what I cooked for them, but they were welcoming and grateful. At that time, I liked her, but she had some of the best parents. I refer to them as *Moms and Pops*. Alicia had shared with me that she had a brother who was also battling addiction and in-and-out of prison and from day one, I was always transparent with them about my life, where I had been and what I had done. I was an open book. My stories kept them laughing, but the truth of my stories also sometimes brought tears and pain.

Alicia's father was a preacher, and I had never met a preacher like him. He wasn't rich and he was very sincere in his ministry. He wasn't in it for the flash and the fame. Our bond is natural and having been addicted to drugs myself has allowed me and Pops to have some transparent conversations about the nature of addiction and what his son was going through, and I've been able to open up to him and Moms about anything and everything that I have gone through. Her father and I have developed a bond that would last a lifetime. What we have developed in special. He is a voice of reason for me and I have become a caretaker and acted as a son for him.

During the time that I came into the picture, Alicia's sister had begun her vegetarian journey. Today, she's a hard-core vegan but back then, she was a vegetarian and could still have tortellini. I prepared a full menu,but since her sister didn't eat meat, I prepared a few special dishes for her. I had deboned an entire turkey, prepared greens, candied yams, grilled steak, grilled salmon, garlic mashed potatoes and more.

Everyone sat down to eat prior to her getting there and had already had round one and some of them, like her son, his girlfriend, Moms, and my friend were all relaxed and in TV mode. I went into the kitchen to cook her tortellini fresh and to plate the rest of her food. She sat down at the glass round dining table thinking that she was going to eat alone and in total solitude, but Pops took a seat at the table and he became interested in her special dishes and began to gaze at her delight in eating it and throwing me questions about it.

Alicia's sister sat there focusing on her meal and looking unbothered as Pops said, "That looks good." She didn't break a sweat at him after hearing the comment. Alicia and I fell forward laughing. We knew that Pops was probably thinking that she would suggest that he taste it, but she did not! Pops wasn't the only onlooker, her son's girlfriend who was then eating for two walked by and spotted the tortellini, but she was a little more direct in her quest.

She said, "Chef, do you have any more *tor-doe-dinis?*" She tried to pronounce it correctly and of course, I obliged and fired up the stove for another a few servings. I didn't want Pops to miss the experience and I couldn't deny a pregnant woman her food.

As I was moving around the kitchen quickly, I started so good and confident that I forget that my body was in recovery and I went into a fall that felt like it was happening in slow motion. I just knew I was going to hit the floor and then all of a sudden, the son's girlfriend, *"Ms. Tor-doe-dinis"*, pregnant and all, stepped in for the save and kept me from hitting the floor.

We celebrated Thanksgiving at Alicia's grandmother's house. Her mother's side of the family had gathered to eat dinner and everyone was assigned to bring a dish. Alicia and I were responsible for the turkey. We had gone to meet Mom and Pops to pick up the turkey and so that I could work my magic with my deboned turkey. I made my gravy from the bones and the other leftover things and also cooked the stuffing inside the turkey.

Her extended family wasn't familiar with me at this time so I came in low-key. I wasn't Chef today, I was just Terrance, who had prepared a meal. Moms walked past me and grabbed me making comments that her sister-in-law was using a lot of salt in the instant mashed potatoes. I pointedly didn't make any comments. Pops asked her in an irritated manner, "I thought you were going to bring the mac and cheese?" She tried to explain that she was told the mac and cheese was already spoken for and handled.

After seeing a little struggle in the kitchen, especially with the mac and cheese, I stepped into the kitchen and asked if they needed any help at the same time as Alicia said, "He's a chef."

Her uncle immediately asked, "Why didn't you say so sooner?" And with that, I washed my hands and jumped in and I reworked the mac and cheese. They devoured the turkey, stuffing, and gravy and her uncle almost hurt himself on that gravy.

One night I couldn't sleep because of the pain and I was up late. I had been looking for my dad and my dad's side of the family for my entire life and something told me to post about it on Facebook. I don't know why I did it, but I wrote a post asking if anybody knew Sam Dorsey, my father. I don't think I was looking for him particularly, I was just looking for his family because I was tired of my mom's side of the family that I had been raised by. Lo and behold, my prayers were answered. Somehow, my post was shared and made its way across the internet until it was seen by my dad's brother, my uncle, who was living right in the same city in Virginia! I couldn't believe it.

It was like my own Antwone Fisher story. He called and asked if he could come meet me where I was staying. I was shocked. God really was listening to me! But I didn't want him to see me in my full body cast, so my friend helped me to take off the cast before he came by.

My uncle came through the door of my friend's house and he spent a moment looking at me, then said, "You look just like your daddy." I couldn't believe it. This was really my uncle and I could see that he kinda looked like me too and I felt happy and relieved. We talked for a little bit and he filled in the gaps of information that I had been missing. He told me that I had disappeared from their lives when I was a child when my mom had basically kidnapped me and took me from Alabama to Michigan. My uncle explained that they had been putting pressure on my mom to bring me around my dad's family more, but she didn't want that, so she snatched me up and hid me from them until they gave up looking for me. It was ironic that I moved basically right onto their doorstep in Virginia.

For about three or four days afterwards I was still in shock, processing what I had learned about my family. I had gotten a part time job in the barbershop and one afternoon I was cutting someone's hair and I looked up at the TV and saw my uncle! I hadn't asked him what he did for a living and I only caught the last few seconds of him on this commercial. I told my friend who assured me that I was just seeing things because I was thinking about him too hard.

My uncle called a few days later and invited me over for Thanksgiving dinner with his family. My friend was invited as well and she drove me over to his house. When we pulled up to the address he gave us, there were 7 or 8 cars parked in front of this grand old house. I rang the doorbell and my uncle answered, greeting us warmly and ushering us inside. My friend and I were both in shock looking around at everything and we kept making eye contact, silently asking each other what had we gotten ourselves into!

"I can't believe how much you look like your father!" a woman exclaimed, coming over and grabbing me by the hand. She introduced herself as my Auntie Vee.

"When did he pass?"

"He ain't dead!" she laughed. "He lives right here in Virginia and he works for us!"

"What!?" I was taken aback. "Is he here?"

"We told him you were coming," she shook her head. "But you can come to our place and see him! We work in healthcare."

"What do you guys do?" I asked. "Do you have a commercial?"

"We got about 5 commercials!"

I exclaimed excitedly, "I knew I saw y'all on TV!"

My auntie nodded enthusiastically, "We're Dorsey Extended Hand. We have over 600 people working for us and 25 people that just answer the phones!" She told me that they wanted me to come into the family business.

I was shocked and excited but I stressed to her that I didn't want anything from them. "I've been waiting too long to find you guys and I don't want you to feel that I'm around for your money." That was a feeling that I was all too familiar with. "I'm a chef and I cut hair and I do pretty good for myself! I just want my family, that's the only thing I want."

I hadn't seen Sam, my biological father, the sperm donor, in 34 years. My uncle and auntie had invited me to see the family business, and everybody knew that I was coming to the office except for him. I don't know what I expected and even though my auntie had told me they had six hundred employees I was shocked to see that the office building was the size of an elementary school.

When I walked in, she greeted me and gestured behind her, telling me, "He's back there." I thought with them owning this gigantic medical building, that my father would be someone, maybe in a position of some type of management or administration position. But when I walked up on him, he was dumping the trash next to a freshly mopped floor. I stood there silently, observing him, until he seemed to notice my presence and turned around. Then he just stood there and looked at me. Finally, he broke the silence and asked hesitantly, "Terry?"

"Yeah," I said. "It's me."

"Well, you changed," my father drawled, looking me up and down.

"Yeah, I haven't seen you in some thirty years, so I would hope that I changed." I guess he still viewed me as a little boy. The only other time he'd seen me was when I was 12 and I hadn't seen him since then.

Sam nodded slowly and said, "It's good to see you." Then he turned around and continued tying up the trash bags. For the first time in my life, I truly felt sorry for my mom, and understood that she had made the right decision in taking me away from this stranger who was my father. After that conversation with him I turned around and stormed out the building. I didn't want to blow my top in front of my new family. There was complete rejection right there.

My uncle came to where I was staying and he grabbed me by the hand and said, "Don't let him run you away from us. I don't deal with him, I just let him keep working here because of my mom." Their mother had recently passed away and they were still grieving. He shook his head sadly, continuing, "He ain't shit and I just wanted you to see that he ain't shit so you don't expect much. We want to have you around."

I asked, "Are you sure?"

"Yeah, I'm sure," my uncle promised. "We don't have any kids of our own." I was a new breath of fresh air for the family. I was lively and I didn't need anything from anybody. Right then and there, we made a bond and my uncle and I have been real tight ever since. Auntie Vee is one of the best businesswomen I ever met and she started showing me the ropes. She explained to me how a 501c works and the difference between LLC and non-profit organizations. She taught me so much! I would go up to the office and observe how she walked, looked, and talked, the way she maneuvered through contracts.

It was like a breath of fresh air. I still carry the lessons from my NA meetings, that if I keep going around the toxic members of my family, I would relapse and end up back on drugs, and that thought still scares me, so I do everything in my power to stay on the straight and narrow. I keep minimum contact with my mom's side and set boundaries against them communicating with my dad's side of the family, who accepted me whole heartedly. Through them, I found out I had two other half-brothers and three sisters, one older and two younger than me. All of my biological father's children inherited his strong genes and after reaching out to them and getting to know their stories, I found out that our father practiced being an equal opportunity deadbeat. He didn't do shit for none of us. If you ignore my poor excuse of a biological father, meeting his side of the family has been nothing but love and brought indescribable peace to my heart.

I ended up going down to the unemployment office, since I still couldn't work fulltime and I had to try to get some type of training. I was only doing part part-time at a barber shop helping them when they were overbooked. I still wasn't able to stand up for long periods of time. When I got down there, they told me I was a hurricane disaster relief person and that I was eligible for free Merchant Marine Seaman's training, where you get a license to work on the ocean. "You think I can apply for that?" I asked, informing her about my time in prison.

"As long as you're honest in your application." She pointedly did not look at my body cast. "That training does require a physical, but you might start with theoretical part of it."

The Maritime School let me start the Merchant Seaman's training, doing all the bookwork. My body cast squeaked like I was the Tinman in desperate need of oil, but my classmates were so helpful. My friend would drop me off at the school on her way to work, and some of my classmates would come out to the car and help me get into the classroom. Some of us studied together and I felt alive again and it felt good to know everybody was really nice to me, like they wanted friendship for who I am rather than what I could bring to the table.

When I had been getting my Merchant Seaman License at the Maritime Academy, I asked one of my instructors, "Why don't you advertise the Merchant Seaman training opportunities in the urban communities?" He didn't seem to like me, but I had assumed it was because his approach was rigid. If you came in and disrupted it, trying to do things in a different way, he came down hard – and I was always trying to be creative in the way I learned and handled tasks given to me. Sometimes I had struggled through school as a child and it wasn't until I got to know myself fully as an adult that I figured out I have a learning disability. It was nothing to be ashamed of, I just learned in different ways. I didn't read, I was an audio and a hands-on learner: I learned by memorization and doing.

He replied to me, "We don't want them." I stared at him, shocked, understanding suddenly that it wasn't my work methods he disliked, it was my background. I came from the ghetto, from prison, and I was part of the *them* that they didn't want. Although this opportunity came to me after hurricanes and back surgery, I knew that if I hadn't ventured out of the 'hood I would have never heard about it. It struck a fire inside of me and I was newly determined to finish the training and prove them wrong.

When it was time to graduate, I had to take the physical examination. You have to do the fire training and then you have to do the survival on the water, and then you have to swim for 3 minutes. I started going to the Y, trying to learn how to float again. I knew that the fire suit weighed like a hundred pounds and I could barely hold myself up. I started taking the suit off day by day and walking around with a backpack full of books to build up my strength, then I started walking around with my friend on my back.

On the day of the physical examination, they tried to deny me access. "We can't let you do that yet, Chef. You were just in a full body cast last week; you might be a liability!"

I told them that I would sign whatever paperwork they wanted me to, stating that I wouldn't sue the school in case something happened to me, but still the instructor of the class tried to say that wasn't good enough. "Mr. Wallace, we simply can't let you take the training."

"Please just let me try," I begged. "Let me try the swimming and if I can't do it, you just fail me, okay?"

The instructor looked at me sternly, and then said, "The second I see that you're in trouble, I'm going to pull you out and fail you." They put me in a full body rubber suit and I jumped in the water and gave it everything I had. I was ecstatic to pass that test.

The next day was the fire test. You had to put on this suit that weighed like a hundred pounds. I was walking with my legs spread wide to keep my balance. Then you had to pick up the hose. Everybody in the class was like, *don't make him pick up the hose, don't make him pick up the hose.* I bent over to pick up the hose and it felt like I was trying to lift 700 pounds. I was pulling, sweating, straining for dear life, and then I did it. I picked up the fire hose and I locked in.

The instructor said, "You want to walk over there with the fire hose and spray out the fire." I took the biggest steps that I was capable of and I prayed to the Lord, *I need this job, I need it, I need it.* I passed that test too.

After that, I couldn't move for three days, literally could not move a single inch. It felt like I had pulled every muscle inside me. It was a miracle and an example of pure sheer will power, because even just weeks before I could barely move my own body weight.

As soon as I was physically able, once I had completed the merchant seaman training, I returned to the Virgin Islands to recoup my food truck and my property. It was nothing like it was when I left, a tropical green paradise. Even though it was over six months since the hurricanes hit, the damage was still in plain sight all over the islands. When I walked up to my condominium, the roof was blown down the street and all the windows in my car had exploded. Blue FEMA tarps covering destroyed roofs dotted the mountainside as far as you could see. The tourism industry which supported the island had pretty much crashed. The yachts that made me a good income were no longer working. When I went to Tortola, some of the yachts were in the middle of the street, flipped upside down.

My food truck was flooded on the inside and at first glance, part of me doubted that it would ever be fully functional again. I was barely able to stand up at that point in time, but people back in the states had been calling me, offering to support using my food trucks to feed the community. By the grace of God, after we cleaned it out, everything was still operational. We started trying to feed the kids who weren't going to school because of hurricane damage, and the contractors who had come to rebuild the islands. It was my honor to help feed the community and I did what I could for as long possible.

But the Virgin Islands didn't get the money to pay the contractors, so now the contractors came to the food truck out of pure hunger, because I was the only person over there from the mainland that they knew. I was taking IOUs on good faith and a few of them paid me, but most of them didn't. I stayed for almost five months, but since I wasn't getting paid, my funds ran out. Services for shipping my things back to the states weren't up and running yet, so I had to leave everything – my belongings, my car, my food truck – with friends.

I returned to Virginia to put my merchant seaman license to use. The school that I had graduated from was having a job fair where I ended up meeting the guy who handled all the personnel and assigned jobs for the ships of Maersk Lines, the biggest shipping company in the world. He asked me what I did and I told him I was a chef. We talked for a while about my experience and my past and then he said, "I want you to work with us." He sent me down to the Seafarers International Union Hall, gave me his card and said, "If they give you any problems, you tell them that I sent you."

I took all of my credentials that I had completed at the school and went down to the union hall at SIU. As the shipping manager had predicted, the guy I was talking to had some issues since the union went by seniority and I had just walked in. "The guy I talked to warned me there might be a problem and told me to give you this card if there was a problem," I said. "You can give him a call."

They talked back and forth over the phone for so long that I started to lose hope of working for them. I didn't know the language out there on the water and suddenly I heard the SIU guy saying, "C-book! You, C-book, come here!"

I looked around blankly, expecting somebody else and realized he meant me. "Excuse me, sir, my last name is Wallace."

He explained to me that I was going to be sent out as a Chief Steward, the guy who ran the kitchen and supplies on the ship. I broke the mold. I was the first person in SIU history to go out on the water as a Chief Steward on his first day on the ship. Usually, you have to go through a series of classes and training, but through my various experiences I had all the training and then some. Their own training courses weren't as in-depth as everything I had been through. On top of that, I would make $167,000 a year with ease and I would have full medical insurance. It was an opportunity that was impossible to pass up.

Next thing I know, I'm travelling around the world for my job. I go to Dubai, Bahrain, Pakistan, to Germany and Greece, Japan and Jordan, Saipan and Guam, even to North Korea! The Maersk ships had contracts with the military, traveling out on the ocean. I oversaw this 900-foot vessel. When I walked around it, I felt like I was in charge, feeding over as many as 500 people. One of my deepest regrets is that I didn't join the military and here I am now, working side by side with them and keeping them well fed. It was something I am truly proud of. I have more gratitude cooking for these guys than I had cooking for the celebrities on yachts. I felt that this was my calling.

While working on the ship, I started taking online classes through Stratford University in my down time. A lot of the time we were on the water for days where we couldn't leave the ship to go anywhere or do anything and I absorbed myself completely into learning the business side of the culinary world. I was taking all these certifications: chef manager, chef sanitation, chef beverage manager, hospitality management, the American Hotel & Lodging certification.

A lot of my work history transferred over into college credits and eventually I earned enough that I went to the Stratford University campus in Virginia and walked on stage and I got my associate's degree in Hotel and

Restaurant Management. It was the best day of my life. There were some breaks in my education but I never quit going to school. There were just times when I had to choose work over school to support myself and survive.

As I was sailing and cooking on ships around the world, I started talking to and observing these military guys. There were a couple of guys I noticed who used to get really, really drunk. They would tell me their stories, and I recognized myself in them, using an external rush to try to suppress some internal emotions, all of them stumbling down a path towards addiction. I started talking to them more, trying to take them under my wing and be the mentor to them that I had needed when I was in their positions.

We would work out together, we would talk over things kind of like a support group therapy session. I could see the brightness in these guys' eyes: hunger for something more, and better. I knew that they needed somebody to be a liaison and help navigate away from addiction. I was slowly coaching them through methods I had learned at AA, NA, and the prison programs. These guys would flock to me, wouldn't leave the ship if I didn't go with them out of fear of slipping into old habits. One day, all of them stood up and saluted me, taking their badges off their shirts and handing them to me and giving me these ship coins. These coins were given to the sailors by the captains of each ship for honor or rewards, something like a trophy. It felt so good, I was so happy to help these guys and be a part of this. It felt like I had found the world's best kept secret.

At that time, I was the hottest thing out there on the water. Nobody could cook like me. Everybody wanted me on their ship. Everybody wanted me to come to their companies. People from the yacht agency and the hotels that my buddies worked for around the country would call me up, asking if I needed a job, or knew anyone to send to the hotels. When I started getting good with the military companies, they would call me asking if I would come work for them. Multiple times I had to turn down jobs, telling them, "I'm sorry, I can't be in two places at one time!" But a lot of the guys I had taken under my wing were working for me in the kitchens, and I had been training them to my standards. I started recommending them for the jobs I was offered. They were so good that all of a sudden, I was getting calls left and right, asking for more and more recommendations.

The Seafarers Union didn't accept outside credentials and I was told that I couldn't sail again until I came to their school to take their training program. At first, I was worried that their training would supersede my training, but after I looked into their program, I couldn't believe that they were using a vocational school training program and these guys were making over $100,000 a year. Some of them couldn't cook oatmeal. I was so pissed off that I had taken classes though the American Culinary Federation, the National Restaurant Association, the American Hotel and Lodging, and graduated from Stratford University which gave me a student loan balance/debt in the area of $80,000. If I knew that all I had to do was come to this program, that's what I would have done.

I had the skill set from experience in the industry so I already would have been ahead of the game, but these people couldn't cook their way out of a paper bag. The school's curriculum was copied and pasted from the standards developed by the forefathers of the culinary arts industry Escoffier and Ritz Carlton. These are the legends of the culinary industry who added structure to kitchens and created standards for front of the house and back of the house operations and this Union's school had stripped them of it and relabeled it. There was nothing new under the sun, so almost everything in the industry follows Escoffier and Ritz Carlton's blueprint, but what is problematic is that the Union didn't give them any credit.

After I challenged the school by writing a letter pleading my case for not having to sit through these courses and training, those in power at the school reluctantly agreed to allow me to come to the school and to test out. Companies that wanted to offer me employment had the right to hire so that kind of forced them to agree to this.

As I entered the head instructor's office, I noticed all the credentials that were displayed were from the

American Culinary Federation. I was confused and my first question was, "How do you represent the American Culinary Federation and you got your credentials from them, and you don't accept this credential from students who come into the program?" Even more insulting, their program was a copy and paste from it. The instructor said with a rude look on his face "What you need to understand is that this is our program, take it or leave it." Only a person that had come from formal training would know the difference in what he had done. Even some of the instructors had never been to culinary school. It was a slap in the face for me, but I obliged and took their test. I passed their six-month program in nine days.

How could I walk away from the $140,000 that I could make in nine months? I had never made this much working for anyone and it only required me to make comfort food, not high-end cuisine. I had nothing to lose at this point. This school had a bar in it; this was the first time I had heard of a school that had a bar and it blew my mind. The bar inside the school was the size of a tugboat. It seemed like a set up. So, if a guy failed their seaman test, they would get pissed and go to the bar that was right downstairs and get drunk. I couldn't understand how the school allowed the seamen to get drunk then fail them? What kind of shit was going on here? But I also learned they had their own rehabilitation center around the corner from the school. The game is real and I was down to learn how to play the game.

I called Chef Hill and told him about the best kept secret in the world. I said, "Chef Hill, your prison program was more intense than their program; they didn't even have a cookbook in their school and the material they were learning from was the size of a Jet Magazine." We both laughed.

Chef Hill said, "You should create your own culinary program."

I responded, "Create my own culinary program?"

I never thought of being a culinary instructor, but my new destiny was sitting right in front of my face. I figured if they could do this, I could too, because I was training the guys that just came out of their program. These guys were calling me through Facebook Messenger from different ships around the world asking me cooking questions and techniques. Fast forward three years later and I remember being in Washington D.C. with my family when Chef Hill called me and said, "I've been watching you and you would be the perfect poster child for this new program that is being launched by the industry leaders."

He wanted me to reach out to some professionals in the industry, including state restaurant associations, national credentialing bodies, the National Restaurant Association, and the American Hotel and Lodging Association. I applied to the National Restaurant Association Educational Foundation and my program was accepted to be part of the Restaurant Ready program, a national work-readiness effort.

I had started off washing dishes and I was now a culinary instructor and I began to drop this program around the United States. I named the program, The Turn Around Place (TAP).

PRESENT: TURN AROUND PLACE

I am still a work in progress, but I have some healing and quite a bit of work towards evolution and growth. There is some work that still needs to be done and there will always be work that each of us must do towards becoming the highest form of ourselves. One day, I realized that I could not wait any longer to fulfill the promise that I made to God. I vowed to him during my darkest hour that if he gave me the strength to endure and to come out on the other side of my addiction alive, I would allow him to use me to help others. There were times when I tried to renegotiate my promise. I never did it directly because I would never outright disrespect God in that way. I did attempt to do things my way, but each time I tried, I found myself yielding to His way.

Through all of this, I realized that more than anything, I wanted to help people learn useable, real-world skills. I knew what it was like to struggle through the obstacles that life throws at you and I wanted to help people overcome those challenges. I began building a life in Norfolk, Virginia, with the help from my dad's side of the family. Auntie Vee helped me put together a 501c non-profit organization and we named the program the Turn Around Place (TAP). Eventually we even needed board members! I created a team of people with diverse skill sets: teachers, entrepreneurs, tradesman, and everything in between. These people are dedicated to helping others.

I needed strategic partnerships to really hit the ground running and reach as many people as possible. I approached the city council members and then the county commissioners, who helped me get my program into the unemployment office and partner with the nationwide food bank. The school I graduated from, Stratford University, even wanted to work with my program. I contacted the National Restaurant Association and the American Hotel and Lodging Association. Because my program helps people like me get work readiness skills to enter the hospitality field, I was able to connect to some of their training and credentialing resources. The American Culinary Federation is also part of this as I have all their certificates. The Commissary Kitchen in Virginia partnered with me and together we ended up teaching people how to cook. I ended up putting my food truck there. The Mid-Atlantic Maritime Academy was more than willing to partner with me. We have combined their program with our program where we're teaching people the firefighter training and life-preserving skills on the ships.

The Turn Around Place now has three buildings to operate out of (provided by the Virginia food banks and my family's health care facility) and we did the ribbon-cutting with the city council. We created a job agency and found ways to help people by developing courses in cooking and barbering. Through my aunt's health care facility, we have the industry knowledge to teach in home health care and things in the medical field. I still can't believe all this stuff is happening. Just a handful of years ago I was a guy in prison. Now I'm having meetings with the mayor and the city council and the head of the Department of Unemployment office.

If you are ready in your life right now to get back on track, the Turn Around Place is all about a community where you can take your power back. We provide you with the skills and mentorships to help you in your journey. We've been where you've been. We know what it's like and we want to help you! We offer various classes on improving yourself such as GED training, job placement coaching, culinary training, cosmetology and barbering training. We also offer support in the form of peer support recovery and mental health counseling. We have a staff and team of dedicated professionals ready to aid you in your journey of turning yourself around. You can find us online at www.turnaroundplace.com.

From the corner to the kitchen, my stories are real.

2021 Graduation Day,
Stratford University, Virginia

2021, with Uncle D.

2017 Merchant Seaman's Training, me in the back with a back brace.

2019, Egypt, with crewmates

2020, Philippines, aboard U.S. naval ship

2020, Indian Ocean, with crewmates

2020, Hawaii, with crewmates

WHAT I'VE SEEN THROUGH THESE EYES

Hello, my name is Terrance Wallace

I'm a 35-year-old black man that's been to prison

I know it sounds the same and it's sad

But please give me a second of your time and I'm going to tell you what I've been through the eyes of inmate #374084

I see men trying to figure out the ways of life and trying to understand our downfalls and looking for the right teachings of life

I see men falling prey to the system and having no understanding of life

I see men praying to different gods looking for the rights of life, but this is called what I've seen through these eyes

Some men have different gods looking for the rights of life, but this is called

What I've Seen Through These Eyes

Some men have different gods, lack things in the spiritual value that are willing and get killed and die for them in the name of evil, but this is called

What I've Seen Through These Eyes

I've seen grown men going to school for the first time since grade school facing yet another demon from the past

The goal is called a GED and it's funny I hear some say I don't need that shit I have my GED of the street life but it's hard for me to believe them because he keeps coming back and forth into the system

This is called a fuck-up, the funny word in here they call it a prefix and an A prefix is for the first timer in prison and a Z prefix is where no man has made it before

I feel if we as human beings where granted the gift of eternal life he would keep coming back and forth to the system unit he maxes out to being a Z prefix but this is called

What I've Seen Through These Eyes

It's hard to tell the person who's been in prison most of his life that things have changed for us, as a people, we know deep down inside the odds are against us and this keeps the man fueled with anger and all he can do is point the finger, when you point the finger, you have to be careful because there's always three pointing back at you

They say we as a people must come together and black lives matters, yeah right, the only time we come together as a people is when there a fight or a riot or to press your brother man as you call him for now or to trick him out his jail house goods, its funny

What I've Seen Through These Eyes

You might meet a stone cold killer, a baby rapper, and the so-called big time drug dealer, and, oh yes, let's not forget about the pimp setting outside in the cold rain, trying and laying multiple scam's to slick talk his so-called brother man out of his penitentiary goods, a smoke, or a 25-cent soup, but this called

What I've Seen Through These Eyes

Most men try to build strength by lifting weights but won't lift a book to build their minds so they are mentally weak or has fallen prey to the life of the system

It's hard trying and I say trying again to get you to understand I'm nowhere near perfect but my goal is to be the light in this darkness and I still don't seen the light at the end of the tunnel and hope someone is praying for me and not wishing this madness to stay upon me

All I can do is keep my faith no matter how hard it seem, I know nothing comes easy and if you got it easy I repeat it won't be around for ever but this is called

What I've Seen Through These Eyes

If you got what you got with hard work and prayer, then you have earned that, and this is called

What I've Seen Through These Eyes

It's hard for me to understand how another man has the same love and affection for a man that you would have for a woman, it's seen but unseen heard but unheard and if you ask questions, the reply will be man you must understand the system works two ways it can make or break but me as a man I will stand strong and put my faith in my father not the father that has dropped the seed of birth in my mother womb but the Father from the heaven above some will say there's no father but we both no better and this is called

What I've Seen Through These Eyes

People say the father ain't listening to his prayers, you have to obey the comments that you have made to the father and the woman and kids that you left to fend for themselves, this is the best line of them, babe, if you stick with me this last time I swear to God, when I get out this time, I'm going to this and that, yeah right, you have to obey the commitment you have made to earn that woman love, obeying God laws and man love and keeping your peace with your surrounding and this is called

What I've Seen Through These Eyes

The penitentiary is packed with promise makers, never really understanding the precious time we have wasted and this was called

What I've Seen Through These Eyes